NIGHT

GW01466418

SHITE

Amy Cooper & Debra Taylor

RANDOM HOUSE AUSTRALIA

Random House Australia Pty Ltd
100 Pacific Highway, North Sydney NSW 2060
www.randomhouse.com.au

Sydney   New York   Toronto
London   Auckland   Johannesburg

First published by Random House Australia 2007

National Library of Australia
Cataloguing-in-Publication Entry

Cooper, Amy Elizabeth.
Night o' shite: how to have a good night in with bad movies.

ISBN 978 1 74166 481 2.

1. Motion pictures – Humor. 2. Motion pictures – Social
aspects. I. Taylor, Debra Margaret. II. Title.

791.430207

Cover and text design by Sam Grimmer
Cover stills © Big Australia/Cinetext
Internal stills © Big Australia/Cinetext
Typeset in 9 on 11pt ITC Century by Midland Typesetters, Australia
Printed and bound by Tien Wah Press, Singapore

10 9 8 7 6 5 4 3 2 1

To our mums and dads

CONTENTS

Night O' Shite:
a celebration

Like many of the movies in this book, *Night O' Shite* was born
of indecision, lack of direction and bad casting. It began when
we entered our local DVD shop optimistically hoping to find a
movie that would thoroughly entertain us.

We scanned the shelves for quality, but all we could see was wall-
to-wall shite – here a *Glitter*, there a *Swept Away*, everywhere a
Waterworld. And of course, the mother of all shite: *Showgirls*.
Nowhere in sight was there an enticing Sundance or Oscar winner,
or even a glowing review from someone arty and bearded to help
us. Besides, we'd once been lost in *Lost in Translation* and had
developed an unreasonable fear of navel-gazing. What to do?

Being bone idle by nature, we realised it was easier to take our
chances with a turkey. We plucked the nearest one from the shelf
– it happened to be *Gigli* – took it home, invited some friends
round, and *Night O' Shite* was born.

Very soon, we discovered that shite was not only entertaining
but a bit like a highway pile-up; it unexpectedly brought people
together. We found ourselves refereeing intense debates about
whether *The Postman* was worse than *Waterworld*, whether
Striptease contained more fake body parts than *Showgirls*,
and what on earth Colin Farrell was saying in *Alexander*. We
learned that everyone has a personal league of shite and their own
cherished favourites. Suggestions for inclusion came thick and fast
and we dutifully watched them all, until we earned our reputation
as arbiters of shite.

Through it all, we have come to understand that bad movies
have just as much to offer as Oscar-winning ones. In fact, often
they're more rewarding. You can put aside your expectations,
save yourself the effort of engaging with the characters and stop
searching for those earnest subtexts. It has been liberating to
realise that despite good educations and years of exposure to
critically acclaimed films that should have made us better people,
we remain inherently shallow. With relief, we admitted that
Mississippi Burning and *The Unbearable Lightness of Being*

were not for us, but Travolta's prosthetic forehead in *Battlefield Earth* would bring us endless pleasure.

Not that there isn't a serious side to shite. We have learned much, including: life is more profound in slow motion; if monkeys are in the cast, it's a worrying sign; Paul Bettany needs a new agent; M. Night Shyamalan must be stopped. And in the future, not only will cockroaches always survive, but so will a creature infinitely more troubling – Kevin Costner.

We began to develop the theory that shite is an art form. It's when actors, script, plot, huge budgets and a wardrobe department on the verge of a nervous breakdown all work together to create something so deliciously misguided you can only sit back and marvel at how so many things can be simultaneously wrong.

It soon became clear too that not all shite is made equal. Hollywood now produces so many bad movies that a guide has become a necessity. For true lovers of shite, a film has to be more than merely bad – it has to be appalling enough to provide the basis for an entire night's entertainment. And so many films didn't make our final cut because they just weren't funny or they disturbed or baffled us too much. The also-rans include *Domino*, which made us unwell; *The Hitchhiker's Guide to the Galaxy*, which made us unconscious; *Lady in the Water*, which made us unreasonable, and *Fun with Dick and Jane*, which made us unhappy. Our love of true shite has meant we can't recommend anything that is less than stupendously awful.

We believe the 40 movies in this book will delight you and your friends over and over again. So put aside your shame and reservations and remember: DVD shop staff won't judge you. (When we tried to justify our own bad taste, our local purveyor just smiled and said: 'Don't worry, I've seen it all. I'm like a health professional.') Visit your local store, choose one of our painstakingly selected howlers, assemble your friends and enjoy your own glorious *Night O' Shite*.

Action Shite

FIREWALL

2006

What they wasted:
undisclosed

Minutes you'll lose:
105

THE GUILTY

Director: **Richard Loncraine**
Jack Stanfield: **Harrison Ford**
Beth Stanfield: **Virginia Madsen**
Bill Cox: **Paul Bettany**

TRAILER TRASH

They will make him steal, but he will
make them pay.

The Story

If you must be held against your will, then hope it's by the Firewall School of Luxury Kidnapping. The deluxe package includes your captors doing all the cooking while you put your feet up on the sofa. Even when they storm your house, they politely ring the bell and hand over a free pizza first.

They're all so good-looking and tidy, it's like being held hostage by the gay mafia. Perhaps they just wanted a weekend away, or they don't have families of their own. Maybe a group hug could solve the whole thing.

Sure, they can be a little tetchy, but even when they're trying to prove their ruthlessness they don't turn on you – they just shoot one of their own members. And when they finally decide to bundle you in the back of a van, they're just taking you for a trip on the family boat and even bring Rusty the dog along.

In fact the only real threat is your own fool of a husband constantly trying to thwart your new friends' scam.

While having a rapidly ageing Harrison Ford as your hubby might make for interesting dinner party conversation and provide a scary bogeyman face to frighten your kids into better behaviour, in a kidnapping situation it's a gigantic handicap. There's simply no way of stopping him from trying to prove there's life in the old duffer yet. So while you

He'd nodded off at the wheel again

could be enjoying a few days at home with the kids and some terribly helpful house guests, the silly old coot's facilitating your speedy death by doing absolutely everything the kidnappers tell him not to do.

Why? It's not as though the millions they demand are his own; the cash belongs to the greedy, unethical bank he works for. And even Hollywood's daftest cops would stop short of blaming a chap for trying to protect his family. But no matter how many times the kidnappers politely remind him that geriatric heroics could spell curtains for his perfect nuclear family, Ford just keeps on making a nuisance of himself.

With his body already losing the battle against time, Ford's character tries to race against it, too. Perhaps to accommodate the inevitably ponderous pace of such an unfair contest, the plot hinges on countless improbabilities – not least of all, Ford being able to race at all. While there is something poignant about seeing the man who played Han Solo, Indiana Jones and Jack Ryan still trying to do his own stunts, you can't help but laugh and point.

No wonder chief-plotter Bettany's patience frays. He is well mannered, reasonable and even keeps the regulation nutty gang member in check, but his efforts are rewarded by the bumbling obstructions of a cantankerous grandad. Why do kidnappees have to be so rude?

Delight in the Shite

NO RANSOM BIG ENOUGH

Kidnappers are picky. They exercise a firm preference for sweet, blonde, harmless families. Sadly, this means no-one will ever remove at gunpoint the Osbournes, the Olsen twins (see page 62), your HRT-enraged aunt, any ADHD toddler or even your vicious chihuahua. (The Brady Bunch were ideal kidnap victims, except there was no truck big enough to hold them all.)

WE HEAR YOU, RUSTY

We've suspected all along that Rusty the family dog is the brains of the team and we're proved right when he leads Jack to the kidnappers with his hi-tech GPS collar. Only a smart dog would keep running away from the Stanfield home so often that he needs a satellite-guided restraint.

NICE LIE DOWN

When Jack isn't lumbering around wearing a befuddled expression, he's nodding off. He even manages to snatch 40 winks at the wheel during the climactic high-speed car chase. It's just all too much excitement for an old fella.

KEEP IT SIMPLE, STUPID

Kidnappers' plan:

1 Frame Jack as a gambler
2 Lean on Jack's boss
3 Move into Jack's house for days with more hi-tech gadgetry than Japan
4 Force Jack to fire his secretary
5 Watch Jack all the time – unless he's trying to escape
6 Shoot some of your own gang members
7 Force Jack to hack into all sorts of computers
8 Create a fake affair between Jack's boss and wife
9 Take Jack's family for a trip into the countryside

Our plan:

Seize family, demand money, get money, release family.

Cite the Shite

'You have to do whatever they want. I don't care what it is.'
Beth tries to talk some sense into her doddery hubby

'I'm sick of you people!'
We agree with the kidnapper, and so does Rusty

'My job is taking care of you.'
Wifely affection? Or perhaps Mrs Stanfield knows how old her husband really is

Make a Shite Night of it

A KIDNAPPER ATE MY FAMILY

Go into work, act strangely, steal things, fire people, nod off and then run your boss over. If questioned, explain your family is being held by kidnappers and they are making you do bad stuff.

GRANDAD BOTHERING

Find a grandad, chase him around and see if he stays awake longer than Harrison Ford.

FLIGHTPLAN

2005

What they wasted:
$US 55,000,000

Minutes you'll lose:
93

THE GUILTY

Director: **Robert Schwentke**
Kyle Pratt: **Jodie Foster**
Carson: **Peter Sarsgaard**
Captain Rich: **Sean Bean**
Therapist: **Greta Scacchi**

TRAILER TRASH

She designed the plane from top to bottom.
Now she'll have to tear it apart.

If someone took everything you live for . . . how
far would you go to get it back?

The Story

Jodie Foster doesn't get out much. When she does emerge, it's to work in confined spaces: cellars and prisons (*Silence of the Lambs*); a tiny space capsule (*Contact*), a panic room (*Panic Room*) – and now an aircraft cabin 30,000 feet in the air. This proves something we've suspected for a long time: Jodie Foster is agoraphobic.

You probably would be too if every time you popped outside you were asked to single-handedly turn celluloid turds into gold. How many *Anna and the King*s and *Nell*s does it take before you put on your pyjamas and hide indoors forever, determined never to squander your superior acting skills on shite again?

Not enough, obviously, or Foster wouldn't have gone anywhere near this plane wreck. Maybe the filmmakers wooed her aboard with promises of tiny cockpits and coffins and even squished the movie's title into one made-up word to make her feel more claustrophobically comfortable.

What we do know is that no-one – not Foster or Sean Bean or even their co-star, the amazing giant aircraft with many secret rooms – could avert *Flightplan*'s descent into disaster.

It's another *Panic Room*, except with post-9/11 angst. Just like air-scare contemporary *Red Eye*, it plays on our fear of flying. And thanks to both duds, we're now afraid to go to the cinema, too.

The Pratt family is aboard E474, a futuristic airliner, and they're passengers from hell. Little Julia vanishes mid-flight and Mum (Foster), who happened to design the plane, rampages hysterically around it, upsetting everyone in her path, while she searches for the missing child. Dad's the least trouble – he's downstairs in the hold, travelling home in a coffin.

The flight appears to be a *Lord of the Flies* special charter, with everyone on board – crew included – cruel, selfish or shifty. With this human cargo, you wish the plane would just crash. But it sticks around while the spaces Foster climbs into grow smaller, and the holes in the plot grow larger. Who are the baddies: the flint-eyed captain? The ice-queen air hostess? The obligatory dodgy Arabs in the front row? Or is Foster a delusional nutter swimming in a sea of red herrings?

She was beginning to panic . . .

There is a real villain – but as the success of his evil plan depends upon a series of at least five unlikely events occurring, we never really believe Foster won't make it home in time to sign up for another shite movie set in a tiny space. And as *Flightplan* hurtles towards its daft ending, you can't help reminding yourself that the whole mess could have been avoided if only child restraints hadn't gone out of fashion.

Delight in the Shite

TERRORIST TWITS

Most terrorists keep it simple – bombs, guns, kidnappings – but *Flightplan*'s crims prefer to over-think their evil schemes. The success of this one relies upon several implausibilities, including: Mrs Pratt having designed the plane; none of the 400 passengers noticing Mrs Pratt's child boarding the plane; Mrs Pratt turning hysterical at exactly the right moment; no-one checking with Mrs Pratt's relatives to see if her child really exists . . . and much, much more.

PILLOW TALK

Presumably in the absence of John Edwards, Kyle Pratt pops down to the hold mid-crisis for a chat with her dead hubby. She unlocks his casket with a special punch-in code and, after a one-sided pep talk, leaves the poor bloke's lid open. If he did kill himself, we're beginning to understand why.

ARABIAN SHITE

What happens when Americans panic? As the lights cut out and fear reigns on E474, instead of using their oxygen masks or calming their terrified children, the passengers queue up, *Flying High*-style, to punch the Arabs in the front row.

PANIC: THE SEQUEL

How to save this movie? Re-release it as *Panic Plane*, number two in a Foster movie franchise of suspense movies set in small spaces.

Other projects include:

Panic Toilet
A single mum (played by Jodie Foster) searches for her contact lens in a cramped cubicle. Evil cleaners want to flush her out. Who will survive?

Panic Library
A single mum (played by Jodie Foster) with librarians in hot pursuit, is buried beneath falling books. Will she escape her overdue fines?

Panic Pub
It's last orders and a single mum (played by Jodie Foster) is wedged between two fat men at the bar. With oxygen and time running out, it's a nail-biting race against the clock.

Panic Burrow
A single fox terrier mum (voiced by Jodie Foster) is stuck in a rabbit hole. Can a kindly farmer rescue her before nightfall? (With soundtrack by Randy Newman.)

Cite the Shite

'Hey, are you watching this movie? Not too funny. Course at 36,000 feet, you can't just up and walk out of the theater.'
Oddly enough, Carson isn't addressing the audience

'All children should be made to wear a cowbell.'
A compassionate fellow passenger soothes agitated Kyle

Make a Shite Night of it

HIDE AND PANIC

Just like traditional hide and seek, but better. The seeker counts to ten while one of the other players hides. The seeker must ask the others for clues about the missing person's whereabouts. Every time he makes a wrong guess, he must run around shrieking, as if in panic. For extra fun, the others may choose to pretend the hidden person never existed.

START YOUR OWN PANIC

Choose fun public places to start a panic. You might create, for example, a Panic Supermarket, Panic Salon or Panic Bowling Green.

POSEIDON

2006

What they wasted:
$160,000,000

Minutes you'll lose:
98

THE GUILTY

Director: **Wolfgang Petersen**
The Wave: **The Wave**
Robert Ramsey: **Kurt Russell**
Dylan Johns: **Josh Lucas**
Jennifer Ramsey: **Emily Rossum**
Lucky Larry: **Kevin Dillon**
Richard Nelson: **Richard Dreyfuss**

TRAILER TRASH

Mayday . . .

The Story

Some things are essential if you are going to make an ocean disaster movie. An ocean, for example, and some kind of disaster – an iceberg, a huge white whale, a perfect storm or a Celine Dion soundtrack.

In this case, the disaster isn't the massive wave that capsizes the *Poseidon* but the remaking of an adventure without the adventure bits in it. Luckily, it hasn't got the 'engaging characters' bit in it either, which means you don't have to worry about who is going to make it out and who isn't.

Instead, you can just sit back and take bets on who gets the Shelley Winters 'Sinks Like a Stone' Award. You can breathe easy, your blood pressure quite normal, as our heroes, puffy Kurt Russell and grumpy Josh Lucas, pick their way through the topsy-turvy world of an ocean liner flipped on its head by a freak wave.

You can watch with comforting indifference as the rag-tag bunch of nobodies that Russell and Lucas are dragging along in their testosterone-fuelled wake succumb to various watery fates.

You can relax as a cast that appears to have been bought cheap on ebay goes through the pretence that any of their characters is really anything better than the nameless bloke in a red velour jumper who always had to be beamed down with Captain Kirk in *Star Trek* for the specific purpose of being a casualty of that week's alien.

And so we have the prom-queen teenage girl and her square-jawed college boyfriend, the single mom and her gratingly cute eight-year-old, the stowaway of ethnic origin, the arrogant coward and Richard Dreyfuss as an earring-sporting gay whose evening begins with being dumped by phone and ends when he's dumped in the briny. Just another Mardi Gras for him, then.

If you were Lucas who has the best chance of survival, you'd simply push them all over and run away the first time Russell starts becoming the hero, or the cute eight-year-old whinges, or the teenagers go all doe-eyed, or the ethnic stowaway expresses an unreasonable fear of ventilation hatches, even though they are the only hope of escape (and claustrophobia would, presumably, be quite a handicap for a stowaway).

Instead he just keeps running around, opening doors and

The drains were backed up again

being surprised there is tons of water behind them, then running off in the other direction and swimming underwater to yet another door with yet more water behind it.

The only reason you feel remotely sorry for this lot is that it has all happened on New Year's Eve, and no-one deserves to be drowning on New Year's Eve unless it's in champagne.

Delight in the Shite

LUCKY LARRY'S FIVE-STEP PLAN

Despite the fact the *Poseidon* is a floating NYE party, only Lucky Larry is a bit squiffy. Consequently, he is the first to die which shows just how misguided this movie is; there is no way a drunk wouldn't be able to handle a little bit of upside down-ness. Indeed, the gang's best bet is to follow Larry's lead and raid the cocktail bar because when you are drunk:

1 You can fall over and not hurt yourself

2 You don't mind things being all out of kilter and a little lopsided

3 You find walking as though you are on a boat quite normal

4 You always manage to get home no matter what the obstacles

5 You are used to looking down narrow openings full of water, like toilets for instance. In fact, the only thing likely to throw you is that you can't get a kebab.

THE WAVE

If we were The Wave, we'd be contacting our agent and demanding to know why we got so much less screen time than the *Titanic*'s floater or the *Perfect Storm*'s storm. After all, the only reason to remake the *Poseidon* adventure appears to be better special effects, and yet The Wave is as impressive as a ripple in a bath; it doesn't even get a song.

SIMILARLY WHEN WET

Perhaps it was the darkness, perhaps it was the water, perhaps we weren't paying attention, but the fact all the women in the gang of survivors are brunette makes them hard to tell apart. For a good half an hour after the stowaway died, we were amazed at how quickly Christian got over Jennifer and moved onto another girl in such a small group (until we realised Elena's refusal to slip up a ventilation shaft had done for her in the end and Jennifer was actually still alive). There is some consolation, of course, that no blondes were harmed during the filming of this movie.

SURVIVAL OF THE DUMBEST

Why do people in disaster movies make life so hard for themselves? For instance, when Jennifer discovers a large metal girder is trapping the legs of boyfriend Christian, she immediately hunts down the smallest woman she can find to help lift it. Later, Maggie proves herself to be the world's most careless parent by allowing her small son to suddenly disappear from view. When she finds him, he's managed to get himself into what appears to be a cage with a rising water level. As a mother, not only should she be holding his hand crossing the street, but also when submerged in the ocean with loose electrical wires and the chance of drowning at every turn.

THINGS THAT GO BUMP IN THE NIGHT

Does Dylan have a middle ear infection? Even when the boat is gliding along quite happily, he keeps bumping into people – first Elena and then Maggie. Perhaps he'd seen the first movie and wanted to get some practice in . . .

Cite the Shite

'[they are] rare, they are unpredictable and they are lethal.'
The Captain states the obvious about rogue waves after one has hit

'I'm king of the world.'
(sorry, wrong movie)

'Whoosh!'
The Wave

'You just don't get the nickname "Lucky Larry". You gotta be lucky.'
Lucky Larry shortly before he becomes Unlucky Larry

Make a Shite Night of it

UPSIDE-DOWN TUESDAY
Turn all your furniture upside down and see how long it takes you to get out of your house walking on your hands (you may need some hands feet for this game, see *Aeon Flux* page 134). Do this on a Tuesday.

BUMPS-A-DAISY
Go about walking into as many people as you can. If questioned, explain you were in a boating disaster movie and haven't quite recovered. See if it makes people fall in love with you.

SAHARA

2005

What they wasted:
$US 130,000,000

Minutes you'll lose:
124

THE GUILTY

Director: **Breck Eisner**
Dirk Pitt: **Matthew McConaughey**
Al Giordino: **Steve Zahn**
Eva Rojas: **Penelope Cruz**
Admiral James Sandecker: **William H. Macy**
General Kazim: **Lennie James**

TRAILER TRASH

Adventure has a new destination.

The Story

Hollywood loves a good read and most novelists option film rights quicker than you can say 'Grisham'. After all, when your book's combined with big budgets and stellar casts, what can possibly go wrong?

Just ask Clive Cussler, author of the best-selling Dirk Pitt adventure series. He'd seen his work mauled so horribly in the 1980 bomb *Raise the Titanic* he swore never to allow Hollywood near his stories again. But somehow, 25 years later, Matthew McConaughey persuaded him to option his 1992 bestseller, *Sahara*.

No-one knows what convinced Cussler, but one suspects it wasn't the production team's movie-making credentials. Executive producer McConaughey's CV consisted of chest-baring action roles, and Breck Eisner had directed only one episode of a TV show. Granted, Breck (note that it rhymes with dreck and wreck) is the son of Disney boss Michael Eisner, but sometimes the apple falls a long, long way from the tree.

One can only imagine Cussler's horrified deja vu as his story of desert treasure hunters – despite starring the buffed McConaughey and fluffed Penelope Cruz – flopped like a beached flatfish. The author's $10 million lawsuit against the production company indicated his distress,

They danced as their careers burned

but it apparently wasn't the meagre $7 million box office takings that offended him most. He sued before *Sahara* even opened, claiming the makers had ruined his original story.

'*Raise the Titanic* was bad enough,' Cussler told *Outside* magazine in the US at the time. 'They butchered that movie . . . even though the book was good. It's the same thing with *Sahara*.'

Familiarity with the book isn't necessary to appreciate *Sahara*'s supreme awfulness. This movie is an entire textbook on how not to make an action flick. It bungles every device successfully employed by Indiana Jones and other adventure classics so ferociously one wonders if Eisner harboured a grudge against movie audiences. Maybe his father forced him to wear Mickey Mouse ears until he came of age. Perhaps he was left home alone with Donald Duck. While you speculate, enjoy *Sahara* – a masterpiece of swashbuckling shite.

Delight in the Shite

DREADFUL DUO

Steve Zahn, already saddled with the unenviable task of playing comedy sidekick to Matthew McConaughey's torso, gets the lamest catchphrase in movie history: 'Hi! How are ya?' The funniest thing he does during the entire movie is lose his baseball cap, which provides his secondary catchphrase: 'Have you seen my hat?'

WHAT ARE THE CHANCES?

Sahara doesn't just ask us to suspend our disbelief – it requires us to hang it by the neck until dead. We found it especially inconceivable that . . .

• Penelope Cruz, doing full-volume Latina glam and with an accent more impenetrable than the Amazon jungle, is a senior World Health Organization official 'specialising in plagues'
• Penelope Cruz's character, Eva Rojas, knows where to source a designer evening frock, make-up and hair products in remotest Mali
• Dirk Pitt, despite being unable to do up his own necktie, is an ex-Navy SEAL
• Anyone would walk even as far as the corner shop to search for this worthless old wreck
• These clowns could make a windsurf machine out of an old, wrecked plane
• Hairy, short Steve Zahn is not really Bill Oddie.

WATCH YOU DON'T TRIP OVER THAT WARSHIP

What are the chances of stumbling across a buried US warship in the 10-million-kilometre-wide Sahara desert? The odds, according to bookies we consulted, are so vast it's not worth a bet. But somehow, our blundering heroes and their target manage to coincide with ease.

DESERT DISCS

The soundtrack, a selection of Americana soft rock, sounds suspiciously like McConaughey's CD collection on shuffle. But while 'Sweet Home Alabama' might make sense during a late-night, nude bongo-playing session, it adds nothing to sweeping footage of the Niger and its exotic surrounds.

Cite the Shite

'He puts the "war" into warlord.'
And McConaughey puts the 'abs' into absurd

'You get the girl, I'll get the bomb.'
Zahn tells McConaughey to take Pen on a date while he picks up his copy of *Sahara*

'We need to re-evaluate our decision-making paradigm.'
Dirk Pitt – or the movie's makers realising their mistake too late?

Make a Shite Night of it

WHAT'S IN THE FACTORY?

Have fun guessing the mystery product being manufactured in the top secret desert factory, then see if you can make one from random household objects.

VILLAIN ROLE PLAY

Ask yourself (in the words of Penelope Cruz's character): What would you do if you were about to be exposed as the worst polluter of modern times?

Award prizes, such as a set of bongo drums, for the most creative answer.

SAHARA TREASURE HUNT

Before screening *Sahara*, bury things in your garden. Split your guests into teams of hero and comedy sidekick, and compete to find the hidden treasure. Note: the treasure does not need to be useful.

THE CAVE

What they wasted:
$US 10,000,000

Minutes you'll lose:
93

THE GUILTY

Director: **Bruce Hunt**
Jack: **Cole Hauser**
Tyler: **Eddie Cibrian**
Kathryn: **Lena Headey**

TRAILER TRASH

There are places man was never meant to go.

The Story

The Knights Templar must feel severely overworked; since *The Da Vinci Code* (see page 24), they've been a must-have in any plot, a bit like a character arc – only in tunics.

While *The Kingdom of Heaven* and *King Arthur* just about get away with claiming a connection, when movies such as *The Cave* toss them into the mix, you realise just how much the enigmatic sect is being misappropriated. It's a bit like the Salvos being implicated in *Debbie Does Dallas 2*.

If the Templars still exist, they should dust off their armour, charge through Los Angeles and take Hollywood by force. We'll help them.

Unfortunately, they'd be too late to prevent their name being bandied about in this tale of unfeasibly glamorous pot-holers poking around a remarkably deep cavern in Romania. Sadly for them, being good-looking doesn't impress a bunch of beasties who pick off any comers to a Templar treasure hidden under a 13th century abbey.

The scene is set for tension and frights, but instead you spend much of your time wondering why the world's best-looking cave-diving team is comprised of the blind leading the partially sighted. In wet suits.

As one of the team remarks, 'I haven't seen a hole like this in a long time,' and, indeed, gazing into the plot of *The Cave* evokes similar feelings of wonder and awe.

For instance, as the strange collection of monsters slowly emerges, it becomes clear that the pot-holers' predecessors weren't Templars at all, but evil members of Jim Henson's Workshop. This is confirmed when one of the cavers is attacked by what looks suspiciously like a hand in a sock with some dentures stuck on it.

Other cave-dwellers include a huge eel that only leaves behind the shoes of its victims (admittedly, an eel wouldn't be needing footwear), and a massive flying bat that looks a bit like Sigourney Weaver's adversary in *Alien*, if it had been a keen hang-glider.

What makes it all so fun is that the attractive pot-holers won't just die painful and unpleasant deaths if they get bitten, they slowly turn ugly. It's comforting news for anyone who isn't unfeasibly glamorous and, probably, a massive relief to Knights Templar everywhere.

Delight in the Shite

ADOPT THE JACUZZI POSITION

Besieged by vicious predators and slimy things under the water, the world's best caving team has cleverly developed a defensive position in which they link arms and form a circle, just like a synchronised swimming team. You really wouldn't trust these people to get you out of a spa bath, never mind a life-threatening situation.

CREATURE COMFORT

Why does no-one in adventure movies ever find previously undiscovered friendly fluffy creatures, a lost species of Maltese terrier or an unclassified branch of the koala family that just wants someone to hug? Instead, there's always something resembling a vindaloo with teeth that's very, very angry.

PICK OFF THE WEAK ONES AT THE BACK

If you are considering leaving the comfort of your sofa to pot-hole, make sure you have the standard issue action team:
• A stoic leader who thinks laughing will make him weak
• A reckless wannabe who thinks being stoic will make him a laughing stock
• One person from a minority

'I haven't seen a hole like this in a long time . . .'

- An older, philosophical man
- A tomboy who looks good in a sports bra
- A beautiful but intelligent girl
- As many cannon fodder at the back as you like.

THE MOLE

All the creatures are deformed hybrid humans yet when the cavers first encounter trouble it comes in the form of a ferocious mole-like creature. Did the Templars originally take a midget with them?

SLOW-ACTING MONSTER

While everyone around him starts morphing into a monster straightaway, Jack fends off the impulses until the end of the movie. What is his secret? Vitamin C? Or perhaps it's in the genes as Tyler is similarly resilient, making it to the outside, where he ominously suggests to Kathryn that he's got the bug and now he's loose. Or perhaps that horrified look on her face is because she's realised there could be plans for a sequel.

Cite the Shite

Memorise the world's greatest dive team's drinking salutes:
'Respect the cave!'
'To Virgin caves!'

Make a Shite Night of it

FUN KNIGHTS IN

Get a copy of a movie guide like Leonard Maltin's, open it randomly and put a pin in the page. No matter what movie you've chosen, try to work the Knights Templar into the plot. Extra marks if you can introduce a hand puppet, too.

SPA & SURVIVE

With your friends, practice the Jacuzzi Position until it becomes second nature. It might save your lives one day.

THE DA VINCI CODE

2006

What they wasted:
$US 125,000,000

Minutes you'll lose:
149

THE GUILTY
Director: **Ron Howard**
Robert Langdon: **Tom Hanks**
Sophie Neveu: **Audrey Tautou**
Jacques Saunière: **Jean-Pierre Marielle**
Sir Leigh Teabing: **Ian McKellen**
Silas: **Paul Bettany**

TRAILER TRASH
Seek the truth, seek the codes.
Break the codes . . .

The Story

*T*he Da Vinci Code is a true miracle of holy shite. First of all, through benign intervention, it takes a mediocre novel and transforms it into a long cinematic cliché of biblical proportions that quickly brings you to your knees in awe.

Then it smites Europe down with a plague of comedy foreigners, many of whom appear to be reading from the gospel according to 'Allo 'Allo, and ordains that Hanks must become a movie martyr, prostrating himself on the altar of the Church of the Badly Cast without any thought for his own salvation.

And then it takes one of the most controversial theological theories of all time and makes it so astonishingly dull, the revelation that *Touched by an Angel* didn't really have angels in it is far more likely to shake the foundations of your belief system.

Once you witness all of this, you will be forced to question why anyone ever had any faith that the movie of Dan Brown's hugely successful but deeply flawed yarn might actually be any good once it was put in the hands of Ron Howard (whose other great religious works include *How the Grinch Stole Christmas*).

With the unrelentingly wholesome-but-dull Howard at the helm, the pace and urgency of Brown's thriller sinks quicker than someone who can't walk on water. For example, on paper, you can just about get away with a limping albino monk wrapped in nothing but Friar Tuck's hand-me-downs turning up unnoticed in densely populated European cities, committing murders and indulging in a spot of self-flagellation.

On screen, however, Bettany's pale-eyed, peroxided nutter is to unseen assassins what Maria Von Trapp is to nunneries.

On paper, Sophie (Tautou) continually asking questions is a useful device, on screen you can't help but think she must be the only person in the Western world who *hasn't* read Brown's theories.

Spot the painting!

On paper, the Priory of Scion seems a mysterious and powerful band of believers. On screen, they rock up looking like a few dodgy Scottish village market stall owners and some old dears who run the local charity shop. They might help you shift some unwanted jumble, but the chances of saving you from Opus Dei are remote – especially as auld Mrs McTavish can't be too far from the toilet.

What we're left with is one long explanation of something we all already know (Holy Grail = cup = wimmins' bits = Mary Magdalene + Jesus = little baby Jesuses = the Pope is wrong = a lot of red-faced clergy), and that makes for a plot thinner than Ron Howard's hair. Still, it's more fun than a red hot poker. Possibly.

Delight in the Shite

WORLD'S BUSIEST DYING MAN

Despite being fatally wounded, Jacques Saunière gets more done in his dying moments than most of us do in a week, running around the Louvre, daubing cryptic messages on walls and floors, discarding his clothes and finally signing off with some particularly complicated self-mutilation. Fearing the phrase 'I'll sleep when I'm dead', Saunière completed as many chores as he could but, unfortunately, failed to vacuum, put the trash out and leave a perfectly clear, understandable explanation on someone's mobile. Old Jacques, bless him, he did like to make a fuss.

FLASHBACK, WHAT A FEELIN'!

See *The Da Vinci Code* and leave your imagination at the door! Yes, there's no need to wonder what might have happened in the past when you use Flashback. Confused about who this Jesus bloke was? Replay the crucifixion all over again! Finding it hard to picture Robert being trapped down a well as a child? Never fear, Flashback comes with a well *and* a child down it – for FREE. Added bonus, this movie only, Mary Magdalene giving birth – just in case you weren't sure what a woman having a baby looks like! Flashback – you'll never have to imagine again.

GOD OF WRATH

Forget all kind acts and godliness; judging by Sophie, the descendants of Christ are an angry lot given to random acts of violence. Despite Silas being on the floor after Teabing whacks him in his spiked metal leg garter, Sophie rushes over to slam the albino's blond head on the ground a few times. Later, when Silas is tied up, she can't help slapping him around a little. Her only vaguely god-like behaviour involves calming Robert's nerves by squeezing his head. What next? Beating the meek with loaves?

EYES WIDE OPEN

It's no wonder Sophie has developed violent tendencies. In one of the many flashbacks we see little Soph peering through a window to witness grandpa Saunière making free with a lady at what appears to be the *Eyes Wide Shut* orgy (see page 116). What we don't see is little Tom Cruise, peering through the other window, equally distressed that old Jacques has managed to get lucky and he can't even get in.

Cite the Shite

'I've got to get to a library . . . Fast!'
Robert remembers an overdue fine

'There was every orb conceivable on that tomb.'
Robert clearly spent his summers conceiving of every orb imaginable. Or taking drugs

Make a Shite Night of it

I'M A CELEBRITY CLERIC, GET ME OUT OF HERE

Each of your friends must dress up as a celebrity cleric – the Pope, Bishop Desmond Tutu, an ayatollah, the Vicar of Dibley and so on – and agree to stay a month in a remote abbey being watched via CCTV by your atheist mates. Each of the clerics must perform a series of miracles – turning water into wine, curing a leper, posing with Bono – before they can be voted Celebrity Cleric!

CHRIST. ALIVE?

Keep an eye out for any descendants of Christ. These may include French women, people in small Scottish villages, anyone who isn't a pontiff and people with beards (Richard Branson, for example). If you find one, *never tell a living soul.*

Epic Shite

A KNIGHT'S TALE

2001

What they wasted:
$US 41,000,000

Minutes you'll lose:
132

THE GUILTY
Director: **Brian Helgeland**
Sir William Thatcher: **Heath Ledger**
Count Adhemar of Anjou: **Rufus Sewell**
Lady Jocelyn: **Shannyn Sossamon**
Geoffrey Chaucer: **Paul Bettany**
Kate the Farrier: **Laura Fraser**

TRAILER TRASH
A funky modern take on medieval times!

The Story

It's a theory that worked well for *Gladiator*: once you've mined every modern sport for movie material, you start on the ancient stuff. But while strapping men fighting to the death makes for great big-screen spectacle, jousting is about as captivating as a tin of peas.

Essentially it is two grown men, rushing towards each other with big sticks, unfairly involving innocent horses in their dumb game of medieval happy slapping. When you've seen one man galloping along with a big wooden pole, you've seen them all, and perhaps realising this, the makers of *A Knight's Tale* decided to jazz up the world's dullest spectator sport with pop songs, some embarrassing dance sequences and a tournament groupie sporting hair that's lost its own joust with crimpers and a silly hat sourced in Jesters R Us.

By this time, it must have seemed a mere trifle to throw in a naked, beat-poet version of Geoffrey Chaucer – who must be turning in his grave so violently he's tunnelled through to Australia – and a girl blacksmith who carves the Nike logo into the armour she makes for our hero, William Thatcher (Ledger).

The result? Not the 'funky modern take' on the Middle Ages but a medieval monstrosity.

The expression of incredulous contempt worn throughout by Rufus Sewell as villainous Count Adhemar says it all. And when Christopher Cazenove, playing Ledger's blind father, weeps uncontrollably, we suspect the tears are real and that he's just discovered it's too late to prevent this abomination from appearing on his showreel.

Much of the enjoyment in *A Knight's Tale* comes from imagining how on earth its various daft concepts were originally pitched. Who in their right mind, on hearing there would be scenes of medieval dancing to David Bowie's 'Golden Years' and football chants such as 'he's blond, he's pissed, he'll see you on the list,' would have green-lighted any part of this pantomime? Luckily for lovers of shite, someone did, and now we have the pleasure of relishing one of the silliest ideas ever to find its way into our cinemas.

A Knight's Tale is the movie equivalent of someone falling over in the street; you know you shouldn't laugh at something

When mullets collide

so unfortunate but you can't help it, and you do so with a delicious frisson of shame.

Delight in the Shite

ROCK SCHLOCK

In an early indication of the shite that is to follow, the film opens with crowds at a jousting tournament singing Queen's 'We Will Rock You'. And thus begins one of the movie world's most inappropriate soundtracks: 'The Boys Are Back in Town', 'We Are the Champions', 'Further Up the Road' . . . It's like the producers bought up big in a 'soft rock songs' sale and were quite determined to use them. Or perhaps Matthew McConaughey just let them borrow his iPod (see *Sahara*, page 16).

DON'T KNOW MUCH ABOUT HISTORY

All that redeemed the real Middle Ages was its lack of football chanting, Nike and unfunny stand-up comics. In bestowing all this upon the period, the movie paints a historical portrait more horrifying than Jocelyn's haircare routine.

BETTANY–NO!

When terribly British, terribly tall Paul Bettany first arrived on our screens, anyone who feared Hugh Grant's best years were behind him felt all would now be well. Perhaps that's why Bettany has become a repeat shite offender, by giving us an albino monk with a love for self-harm (*The Da Vinci Code*, page 24), the world's nicest kidnapper (*Firewall*, page 2), and now Chaucer, stripped bare and rhyming like the *Rent* cast (see page 176). He must be stopped.

HATE AT FIRST SIGHT

Why exactly does Adhemar take such an instant dislike to Will? Granted, he is an annoying backpacker-haired upstart who hangs out with a gang of friends that, when not bickering, are prancing around to Queen songs or encouraging Geoffrey Chaucer to talk gibberish. Actually, Adhemar has a point . . .

Cite the Shite

'Well then, a fox you shall be until I find your name, my foxy lady.'
Sir William invokes Basil Brush

'Geoffrey Chaucer's the name, writing's the game.'
Paul Bettany thinks he's in *Rent*

'He's blond, he's tanned, he comes from Gelderland . . .
And we wish he'd go back

Make a Shite Night of it

HEADS OR TALES

Invite friends round to watch the movie on the proviso they wear a lampshade on their head à la Lady Jocelyn. The person who makes the poorest effort has to create an entire Canterbury Tale – rhyming and all – on the spot. Period clothes optional.

JOUST

Invite a friend round and run at them with a stick.

ALEXANDER
THE DIRECTOR'S CUT
2004

What they wasted:
$US 150,000,000

Minutes you'll lose:
158

THE GUILTY
Director: **Oliver Stone**
Alexander: **Colin Farrell**
Olympias: **Angelina Jolie**
King Philip: **Val Kilmer**
Hephaistion: **Jared Leto**
Cassander: **Jonathan Rhys-Meyers**

TRAILER TRASH
The greatest legend of all was real.

The Story

True aficionados of shite will instinctively know that if you want a truly memorable viewing experience, you must choose a movie that fails to boast one positive press quote on its DVD cover. Add the chilling words 'director's cut', and you can be confident of a (very long) evening of woeful 'artistic' choices.

Notable in the 'director's cut' genre is Oliver Stone, who never believes that studio bosses and financial backers know when celluloid should end up on the cutting floor – and stay there. Instead, the minute his movie has flopped at the box office, he's back in the editing room going through the bins and sticky taping rejected scenes back into his latest oeuvre.

Alexander – The Director's Cut is testimony to Stone's complete self-belief, because only a version that cut out all of the scenes except the end credits could save this embarrassing mish-mash of history, ham acting and Irish accents.

Yep, we said Irish – or more accurately Oy-rish – accents. It's a little known fact that Alexander the Great and all his Greek mates actually hailed from the Emerald Isle.

Faced with star Colin Farrell's thick Dublin slur, it appears

The world's first girl band

Stone took the extraordinary decision to instruct the rest of the cast – including Val Kilmer's King Philip and Jared Leto's Hephaistion – to adopt Oy-rish brogues, which generally wander anywhere between Dublin and the Punjab in their accuracy.

And so we learn that Alexander's wholesale conquering of Asia was, in fact, the work of a bunch of brawling paddies wearing eyeliner and sporting footballer hair who did it for the craic. All of which makes the story of Alexander so much more fun than the boring truth.

The director's take on the invasion of Persia retells it as the world's biggest pub crawl. Philip and Alexander's falling out is, really, just another Irish wedding where someone insults someone else's mother. To be sure, to be sure or, as the ancient Greeks used to say, to be sure, to be sure.

Delight in the Shite

MULLET O' TIME
Stone has never been one to worry himself unduly about chronological order but he overcomes the potential for confusion here by using the little known filmic device – the Time Mullet. Hence, as we zip about from '10 years earlier' to present time, to '10 years later', we know exactly where we are by the length of Alexander's golden wig:

• Short, tight curls – his troubled youth
• Shoulder length, bouncy and manageable – his conquering years
• Waist length, split ends – towards the end of his short life.

It's a complete hair-story of Alexander . . .

THE GIRL'S GOT GUTS
Much controversy surrounded the movie's treatment of Alexander being overly in touch with his feminine side, but Stone seems to tippy-toe around it, bar Farrell and Leto's longing looks. They're probably just wondering who's buying the next round.

THE MUM BEHIND THE MAN
No wonder Alexander is all mixed up. His mother likes snakes, claims to have shagged Zeus and from lengthy calculations conducted with our own fingers, is just one year older than her famous son. Added to this is her idea that a motherly goodnight is forcing

him to hold a python. It's amazing he's as well adjusted as he is.

CUT! AGAIN

On the DVD for Stone's director's cut, there may not be any press acclaim, but there is a little sticker with some big ideas: 'Newly inspired, faster paced, more action packed!' Inspiration, pace, action – they must have been all the things Stone completely forgot to put in the first cut. Good job he got this second chance . . .

HORSE WHISPERER

One of young Alexander's talents appears to be horse whispering – he tames a wild stallion by muttering sweet nothings in its ear. Presumably, it is an Irish horse and can actually understand 'do you want some oats' in Gaelic.

Cite the Shite

'A king must know how to hurt those he loves. It's lonely. Ask anyone.'
Ask anyone who is a king, presumably

'In my womb I carried my avenger!'
Why can't Olympias have a handbag like other women?

Make a Shite Night of it

REWRITE HISTORY! LITERALLY

Pen a thesis on one of the following theories:
• Napoleon was born in Canada
• Vlad the Impaler was originally from Wollongong
• The Vikings hailed from Nigeria.
   When you have finished, send it to Oliver Stone and ask him to make an inspired, fast paced action movie from it. Wait for the cheques to come rolling in.

YOU'RE THE VOICE, TRY AND UNDERSTAND IT

For the duration of the movie, each person in the room has to choose a different accent to their own. The person who doesn't accidentally slip back into their own accent wins a Mullet O' Time wig.

KING ARTHUR

2004

What they wasted:
$US 120,000,000

Minutes you'll lose:
130

THE GUILTY

Director: **Antoine Fuqua**
Arthur: **Clive Owen**
Guinevere: **Keira Knightley**
Lancelot: **Ioan Gruffudd**
Cerdic: **Stellan Skarsgård**
Bors: **Ray Winstone**

TRAILER TRASH

This spectacular motion picture fuses historical grandeur with edge-of-your-seat action and bestows must-see entertainment!

The Story

As yarns go, the legend of Camelot is history's most cracking. For centuries, its universal messages and enduring appeal have inspired great writers to retell the timeless myth. Such is its power that none has ever meddled with the plot.

And then along came Jerry Bruckheimer and his team, and decided they could do better.

They bring us 'the untold true story that inspired the legend'. But in their eagerness to outdo lesser Arthurian storytellers such as Sir Thomas Malory and Chrétien de Troyes, they've overlooked the crucial reason why the true story remains untold: it's crap.

According to this movie, the Knights of the Round Table were really a rag-tag band of tedious losers. They had terrible personal hygiene and instead of gallantry and chivalry, were motivated only by a desire to get home in time for tea. If they really did exist, this sorry bunch must still be laughing in their tombs at how they became the stuff of legend. Maybe Merlin was their spin doctor.

It's actually stunning to behold the reverse alchemy being worked upon history's ultimate human interest story, transforming its solid-gold combination of love, betrayal,

Murder on the dance floor . . .

conflict and tragedy into dross.

Gone are the drama, the charismatic heroes, the magic and the epic love triangle. In their place is a posse of B-listers unable to agree on a common accent or whether they're in a heist movie, a Western or an encounter group for nervous travellers.

Clive Owen's Arthur and his pals are 'Salmations', which makes them the Salmation Army. But with their ratty hair and mucky faces they're more like the Dirtier Dozen, bickering and toilet-talking their way through one last job for their Roman bosses – a trip to liberate a Saxon village in Scotland. On their way they rescue Guinevere, who in this universe is a posh-accented Pict played by Keira Knightley. While the others are as rough as guts, she appears to be from Surrey.

With Ioan Gruffudd's Lancelot a tetchy under-achiever, Arthur a whingeing introvert with emotional baggage and bouffy Italian hair, and Ray Winstone reprising his time-and-place-transcending jolly-cockney-pub-landlord persona, the heroes are more like a poorly motivated group of middle managers on an outward-bound course; or one of those historical reconstruction clubs where bored suburban blokes put on costumes and wave plastic swords.

Beneath absurd beard and hair is our villain, a Celtic maniac who grimaces a lot and growls things like: 'Burn it all!' and 'Kill him!' It's actually Stellan Skarsgård, but sounds just like that voice-over man from trailers for movies like this one. Perhaps it *is* that voice-over man, and he's the true story behind the legend of Stellan Skarsgård. Anything seems possible when you're watching shite of this calibre.

Delight in the Shite

JAILHOUSE SWOT

Despite spending her life incarcerated in a Saxon nutter's tiny dungeon, Guinevere displays all the hallmarks of a very good education. Her plummy vowels and nice table manners suggest a correspondence course. Or that we'd all get ahead if we spent our formative years alone in a small, dark space (see Jodie Foster, page 6).

DRESS CODE DISASTER!

You're about to go head-to-head with hordes of bloodthirsty barbarians armed with broadswords, spears and arrows and, as you'd expect, Arthur's soldiers opt for full-body armour. Keira, however, turns up for the big fight in a teeny bikini and tattoos. We're not sure what she's come as, but she must have received the wrong invite.

DIGITS OF DESIRE
It's the movie's one romantic encounter. For the first time, Arthur is alone with Guinevere. He gazes into her eyes, moves close, takes her delicate hand in his and delivers his kingly chat-up line: 'Some of your fingers are out of place.'

Relax, Casanova. You have nothing to fear.

DIAL-A-BANSHEE
Much of *King Arthur* remains unexplained, but perhaps most baffling are the unidentified crazy ladies who pop up in the final battle scene, screaming, scratching and pulling hair. A possible explanation could be a hens' party gone bad. Or perhaps they're Keira's body-doubles, driven insane by malnutrition.

Cite the Shite

'The Saxons are so close behind my arse is hurting.'

Bors' prophetic bottom saves the day again

'You and I are not the polite people that live in poems.'
But Keira enunciates like one

Make a Shite Night of it

GUESS THE LEGEND
Completely rewrite other epic tales of yore and see if your companions can spot the original. You may, for example, choose to re-work Joan of Arc as a man-eating, selfish atheist or Genghis Khan as a nurse.

TALK DIRTY
Make up your own Arthurian chat-up lines, and then try them out at the pub. Examples to get you started:
• 'One of your knees is dislocated.'
• 'Some of your ribs are cracked.'
• 'You are suffering from type 2 diabetes.'

THE KINGDOM OF HEAVEN

2005

What they wasted:
$US 130,000,000

Minutes you'll lose:
145

THE GUILTY

Director: **Ridley Scott**
Balian: **Orlando Bloom**
Godfrey: **Liam Neeson**
King Baldwin: **Edward Norton**
Tiberius: **Jeremy Irons**
Reynald: **Brendan Gleeson**

TRAILER TRASH

Be without fear in the face of your enemies.
Safeguard the helpless, and do no wrong.

The Story

Why do filmmakers insist on making movies about the Middle Ages? There's just no upside to an historical period that broke out in pus-filled boils during the Black Death, found interesting uses for red-hot pokers during the Inquisition and kicked off the Crusades which eventually led to Dan Brown's *The Da Vinci Code* (see page 24). The entire thousand years were an utter downer.

The opening of *The Kingdom of Heaven* confirms that there weren't any crazy, fun times back then by setting a grim scene – war, repression, poverty, bad weather; indeed, the first shot is the bleak hillside funeral of a young woman whom we later discover has understandably offed herself. But even when you're dead, the Middle Ages can't let you be – the priest has her beheaded to make sure she doesn't just go to hell, but that she'll never find the exit signs, *ever*.

Amazingly, the dead girl wasn't even the unluckiest person in the village – that title is reserved for her blacksmith husband Balian (Bloom). Having lost her and their child,

he's then told by his priest: 'God has abandoned you.' Talk about adding insult.

In the face of such news, Balian's long-lost father turning up and apologising for forcing himself upon his mother and then doing a runner seems the silver lining on the proverbial cloud.

To compensate for years of neglect, dad (Neeson) offers his lad a refreshing break in the Middle East slaughtering infidels – a sort of Kontiki tour for the pathologically violent who want to get into heaven.

Balian, who is feeling terribly glum, can't be tempted until he sets the village cleric ablaze. Dad's offer is better than the hanging, drawing, quartering and then chopping up in thin slices that constituted medieval justice so our humble hero embarks upon an adventure that proves he was wasted as a metal worker.

After just a single two-minute lesson, he is suddenly a master swordsman. With only a few words of advice from his dying father, he picks up good knightship quicker than you can say King Arthur (See *King Arthur*, page 38). When presented with his inheritance – some barren lands – he transforms them into lush paddy fields. Facing a 200,000-strong Saracen army, he shows himself to be a courageous military leader.

You can imagine that Balian must have merely majored in blacksmithing but his other subjects were agricultural irrigation, fencing and military strategy. Perhaps the education system in the Middle Ages was the only thing that wasn't shite.

Delight in the Shite

THE UNLUCKIEST MAN IN THE WORLD

If you saw Balian coming, you'd hide behind the nearest sand dune. Whenever something good happens to him, there's always a downside (see below).

And so it goes on. He even sits on the hill where Jesus was crucified to ask forgiveness but claims 'God didn't speak to me'. No wonder, the Almighty was probably steering well clear in case an anvil fell on him while he was praying.

BITCH-SLAPPING

What is it with knights? Why can't they be nice to each other? Even when the dying Godfrey (Neeson) is bestowing his title and wisdom upon his newly found son, he can't resist bitch-slapping him at the end of his poignant speech. King Baldwin, despite having a touch of leprosy, gets in on the action by giving Reynald a good backhander, while Balian himself passes the slap onto a servant he decides to pronounce a knight. Perhaps if medieval knights had done

On the sunny side	Then again…
His long lost father shows up and is a baron!	He dies of 'marrow seepage' after protecting Balian from arrest
He's told he has land in Jerusalem and heads off to claim it!	The ship sinks
Although he's washed up in the desert, there's a horse!	The horse runs off
He finds the horse and an oasis!	Unfortunately so do two Saracens who pick a fight
He wins the fight!	He's killed a big cheese in Saracen land and is now a marked man
A beautiful woman falls for him!	She's married to a mincing French psychopath
He goes off to find his land!	It's arid

He was dogged by bad luck, and a tall bald man

a little more hugging, there would have been fewer invasions and more parties.

TAKE YOUR TIME

Director Ridley Scott just can't resist letting us see every battle, skirmish or fight in the all-too-predictable slo-mo beloved of epic action movies. It is so overused that, if you only learned from movies, you'd assume throughout the ages all great battles were conveniently slowed down to a more manageable pace so the soldiers didn't get worn out.

YOU'VE GOT TO HAVE A GIMMICK

Blacksmithing is to Orlando Bloom what wolf-like facial hair is to Hugh Jackman – you've gotta have a gimmick in Hollywood these days. Perhaps he went on a metal-working course after he realised there weren't many parts for someone specialising in being Elvish. Having scored *The Kingdom of Heaven* and *Pirates of the Caribbean*, the line in his résumé that says 'can shoe horses' is obviously working for him.

BIG, ANGRY AND GINGER

Brendan Gleeson is perfecting the inexplicably murderous villain. Having played Menelaus in *Troy*, here he ups the ante by making Reynald a ranting, ginger-haired loon who goes about starting wars because 'someone has to'. In between concocting ingenious plans to send the Saracens into a right strop, Reynald appears to spend his time applying henna to his flowing locks to achieve a shade of ginger almost as violent as his moods.

Cite the Shite

'I once fought two days with an arrow through my testicle.'
Must have been a dare . . .

'I am what I am.'
Reynald feels a song coming on

Make a Shite Night of it

THE MAN IN THE GOLDEN MASK
Scott claims Edward Norton is under the mask King Baldwin uses to hide his unfortunate skin disease, but we're not convinced he's in there all the time. It could be anyone. Do research to discover, during the period the movie was being made, the whereabouts of Michael Jackson, Paris Hilton and Mickey Rourke.

YOU CAN NEVER HAVE TOO MANY HORSE SHOES
Enrol in a blacksmithing course immediately. At the very least it will lead to movie roles, at the very best you will become a leader of men.

GO SLO-MO
Do everything in slow motion. See if it makes your life more profound.

THE NEW WORLD

2005

What they wasted:
$US 30,000,000

Minutes you'll lose:
135

THE GUILTY

Director: **Terrence Malick**
John Smith: **Colin Farrell**
John Rolfe: **Christian Bale**
Pocahontas: **Q'Orianka Kilcher**

TRAILER TRASH

Once discovered, it was changed forever.

The Story

Pluck *The New World* from the DVD store shelf on the strength of its swashbuckling cover, and prepare to be shocked. While the packaging promises a rollicking, *Last of the Mohicans*-style adventure story, the film itself couldn't be farther removed from epic entertainment if it were snail porn or a documentary about glass blowing.

Here you will find no Daniel Day-Lewis tearing through the shrubbery, no gallantry or period-piece action, no moustache-twirling hero or dastardly rogue. Instead, we're served a pile of pointless performance art accompanied by a drawling Irish narration from Colin Farrell sounding as if he's at the wrong end of a Friday night bender, reading a script even *Nell* would consider inarticulate.

And yet, because it's directed by the notoriously non-prolific Terrence Malick (lauded by America for having made a masterpiece, *Badlands*, in 1973, he then took 15 years to reappear with the navel-gazing *Thin Red Line*), this load of muttered nonsense and alfresco charades is hailed as genius.

Typically, no-one has questioned why Malick stopped making movies for over 20 years. But *The New World* holds all the clues.

Despite appearing to be a bunch of incompetent lay-abouts who couldn't organise an allotment let alone a colony, the English discover America and immediately go wandering through the long grass, communing with nature and gamely letting the natives blow smoke at them.

This approach works well and everyone is happily getting along in a way that would make Sting proud, until Smith spends a few months at Indian camp and falls for the chief's favourite daughter, Pocahontas.

This presents several obstacles. First there's the lack of a common language, which

When Captain Smith met Pocahontas, they had a very dull affair

necessitates a lot of hand waving. Second Smith insists on fretting about big existential questions such as: 'Who are you whom I so faintly hear?', 'Who urges me ever on?', 'What voice is this that speaks within me?' ,'Where's my beer?', 'Will the bouncer eject me if I order more Jack Daniels?, 'Who am I?' This doesn't really fit with Pocahontas' own hobbies: stroking cows, playing with parrots and chasing butterflies.

Faced with such a cultural clash, Smith and Pocahontas do the only thing that two people who fancy each other but can't communicate or have sex can do – they go for a brisk walk. And they walk, and walk, and walk . . . until you aren't quite sure whether you are watching a movie or just a ponderous, interminable game of 'It'.

Apparently, theirs is a romance that needs no words, although it could be enhanced by a pedometer. And, apparently, Malick is a director who can throw whatever he likes at the screen and expect plaudits. At least *The New World* provokes some important questions, such as 'Why did I hire this?', 'What shite is this that speaks to me?', 'Shall we play charades?', 'Are you "It"?' and 'Where IS my beer?'

Delight in the Shite

THEY THINK IT'S ALL OVER

After what seems like an eternity of Smith traipsing around after Pocahontas mumbling things, he is mercifully sent back to England. Just as we're enjoying the silence, along comes John Rolfe, who immediately starts following her with those all-too-familiar questions: 'Who are you?' and 'What do you dream of?' Poor Pocahontas; she can't nip down to the cowshed without the core of her very existence being questioned.

FICKLE

Believing Smith is dead, Pocahontas agrees to marry Rolfe, only to discover Smith isn't dead at all but is waiting to meet her in London during her famous visit. What do they do after years of separation and anguish? Yep, they take a walk, she sits in a tree, he ponders some unanswerable questions. Then, in a sudden flash of credibility, Pocahontas suddenly realises Smith is a bore and decides she doesn't love him at all. And he's walked all that way . . .

BRAZILIAN INDIAN

While Farrell wears the forest of face fur you'd expect from a pre-Gillette explorer, Pocahontas is suspiciously smooth. While he was bombarding her with all those other questions, you'd think Smith might have enquired how his 'natural' girlfriend came by her shaved armpits and glossy legs. While her people may be strangers to the lawnmower, apparently they were waxing long before the rest of the world.

CONSIDER YOURSELF . . .

When John Smith returns to the colonial camp after his hols with the Indians, the early settlers appear to have been joined by the cast of *Oliver!* Street urchins gather round him, clearly in search of someone to lead them in a rousing chorus of 'Food Glorious Food' – except the extraordinarily incompetent English have failed to plant any crops.

IRISH CONQUER WORLD: OFFICIAL

John Smith was born in Lincolnshire, England – which isn't Ireland. Alexander (see page 34) was born in Macedonia – also not really Ireland at all. Farrell, however, continues on his quest to make us believe all key historical figures hail from Dublin. We can't wait for his Martin Luther King and Ghandi.

Cite the Shite

Pocahontas: 'Did you find your Indies, John? You shall.'
Smith: 'I may have sailed past them.'
A chat about destiny, or is she worried about his smalls?

John Smith: 'Who are you?'
Pocahontas: 'Who are you?'
John Rolfe: 'Who are you?'
Everyone got so bored, they couldn't remember which characters they were playing

Make a Shite Night of it

RAMBLING CLUB

Get a friend to walk a few paces in front of you then begin to follow them, asking questions such as 'Is there a god?', 'Why do we exist?' and 'Where are my undies?' in a whiskey-sodden monotone. See how far you have to walk before you receive answers.

THE MEANING OF LIFE

At one point Pocahontas claims: 'We are like grass.' Discuss. Or don't bother.

Light
Shite

Gigli (2003)
Kangaroo Jack (2003)
New York Minute (2004)
The Prince and Me (2004)
The Terminal (2004)

GIGLI

What they wasted:
$US 54,000,000

Minutes you'll lose:
116

THE GUILTY
Director: **Martin Brest**
Larry Gigli: **Ben Affleck**
Ricki: **Jennifer Lopez**
Brian: **Justin Bartha**
Detective Jacobellis: **Christopher Walken**

TRAILER TRASH
The couple everyone wants to be, in the movie everyone wants to see.

A high octane romance that packs some serious heat.

The Story

Throughout 2003, the Bennifer phenomenon was strangely compelling, like watching a shark attack or a really bad movie – something that clearly hadn't escaped Jenny and Benny, so they headed to the studio to make . . . a really bad movie. Sharks and audiences everywhere braced themselves.

Did we say bad? We meant shite. The movie that Bennifer made was dropped by every UK cinema after a week, boasts the record for largest second weekend drop in box office, and after three weeks disappeared from 2,142 screens in the US. No, not even J-Lo's rear end could save *Gigli* (it rhymes with 'really' – sort of).

And that's why we love it; despite all their clout, the movie Affleck and J-Lo signed up for was as poorly conceived and triumphantly trashy as their real-life romance.

From the moment you read the synopsis on the DVD cover – hoodlum Affleck falls for lesbian Lopez while they mind a kidnapped, mentally retarded youngster – to the end credits, *Gigli* is so stunningly shite, you can only sit back in awe, wondering who gave it the green light and if they still have a career.

But, of course, this isn't just a movie; *Gigli* is a shrine to Bennifer in all its gaudy glory, self-obsession and flashy haste. Like Bennifer, it makes a big song and dance about flying in the face of what's expected, and then winding up nowhere. And, like Bennifer, it is just so damn tacky, you secretly don't want it to end.

Delight in the Shite

ANIMAL FARM

The exchanges between Affleck and J-Lo over the latter's sexuality are what truly put *Gigli* in the Night O' Shite Hall of Shame. Luckily, despite being a pretty simple guy, Larry Gigli has perfected explaining his thoughts on life using animal metaphors. *Old MacDonald had a Farm* was well thumbed in Larry's house. In every relationship, he explains, there are bulls and cows. He is the bull – are you following? – and Ricki (Lopez) is the cow. It's genius. In other philosophical musings, Larry talks of diving for oysters, and even invents his own animals – the dyko-saurus, for instance.

Turkey roll

BATTLE OF SEXES SHOCK: BOTH LOSE

Gigli's finest moment is when Larry and Ricki discuss the aesthetic qualities of the female and male form. While Ricki runs through a series of gratuitously revealing yoga positions, Larry imparts his thoughts on why she shouldn't be gay. Millions of years of genetic engineering, he argues, have gone into fitting man with the right equipment. Alas, it feels like only a few seconds went into writing and directing *Gigli*.

CARRY ON KIDNAPPING

Even if you can ignore the political incorrectness of using a mentally retarded character to get laughs (Look! Someone with brain damage saying 'fuck'), the attempts at bonding between Brian and Larry – who could also lay claim to being 'special' – are ham-fisted.

Despite the fact his captor is constantly threatening him and calling him a retard, Brian falls under the thug's spell once Larry reads him a goodnight story off the label of a bottle of Tabasco. So changed is Larry himself by this, he later refuses to cut the kid's thumb off. Robert De Niro would be ashamed.

GOBBLE, GOBBLE

Ricki's sudden decision to sleep with a man who is two steps up from a chimp is never fully explained, especially considering it's just minutes after she delivers her ode to the female form. Next thing, she's on the bed, legs akimbo, telling poor confused Larry it's turkey time. Romance, it seems, isn't dead. It's living on an Ingham's farm.

Cite the Shite

'If you fuck with the bull, you get the horn.'
Larry revs himself up in front of the mirror

'I am the fuckin' Sultan of Slick, Sadie! I am the rule of fuckin' cool! You wanna be a gangster? You wanna be a thug? You sit at my fuckin' feet and gather the pearls that emanate forth from me!'
Larry was a wordsmith

'It's turkey time. Gobble, gobble.'
Ricki in a romantic mood

Make a Shite Night of it

BULL AND COW TWISTER

Get your friends to draw tickets out of a hat to decide if they are a bull or a cow, and then switch the subtitles on during the yoga scene – cows have to follow J-Lo's moves, while the bulls mimic Affleck's curious hand movements, all the while delivering their respective speeches. Appoint a judge and call him Christopher Walken. When someone gets a move wrong, they have to sing Lopez's 'Let's Get Loud'. Have a drink . . . whenever you need one.

LARRY'S FARM YARD RUN

Sit in a circle and sing a version of *Larry Gigli had a Farm* – each person has to add another animal. If they hesitate or forget previous animals, they have to take a swig of Old Sheep Dippers.

KANGAROO JACK

2003

What they wasted:
$US 65,000,000

Minutes you'll lose:
89

THE GUILTY

Director: **David McNally**
Charlie Carbone: **Jerry O'Connell**
Louis Booker: **Anthony Anderson**
Sal Maggio: **Christopher Walken**
Anna Carbone: **Dyan Cannon**
Jessie: **Estella Warren**

TRAILER TRASH

The story of two best friends who travelled to
the ends of the earth to catch the world's most
unlikely thief . . .

The Story

If Jerry Bruckheimer or Steve Bing ever attempt to enter Australia they should be turned away at immigration – but only after being subjected to a comprehensive cavity search by the clumsiest official available. And if possible, one with enormous hands.

Their tale of two cretins, a rapping kangaroo and some farting camels is an act of aggression towards the Land Down Under only slightly less hostile than a missile bombardment. What did Australians ever do to these men? Movie goers here have always tolerated Bruckheimer's unedifying output and Bing even dated the country's finest export, Nicole Kidman. But watching this movie makes you wonder if Australia once said something really nasty about the producer's mother.

The bulk of *Kangaroo Jack*'s 'comedy' (and there can be no looser definition of the word) is at the expense of poor old Oz, and here are some of the things we're supposed to find funny about the nation: people say 'G'day'; they have different words for 'toilet'; there are kangaroos; the women have breasts.

Billed as both comedy and adrenalin-packed adventure, this pile of emu dung represents the disastrous

Dr Skippy diagnosed halitosis

results of dabbling. It is the first significant contribution to cinema from Bing, otherwise known for fathering Liz Hurley's unfeasibly large baby and denying responsibility. He must have wished he'd done the same with this creation when critics heralded it as: 'crap', 'dreck', 'lethally toxic', 'crass and ugly', '89 minutes of pure agony without a laugh in sight', and 'proof that anyone can make it in the movie business'.

Protagonists Charlie and Louis, a hairdresser and petty criminal, make the *Dumb and Dumber* boys look like Socrates and Solomon. For kicks, they enjoy photographing roadkill and saying 'G'day' – which is how their crazy caper begins. Sent to Australia by Charlie's Mafioso stepdad (Christopher Walken, in an act of supreme self-neglect) to deliver $50,000 to a mob contact in the Australian outback, the lads run over a kangaroo, decide to dress it in Louis' jacket for a hoot, then watch as it wakes up and scarpers with the money in its top pocket.

Their chase around the outback is a catastrophe of clichés, poo and boob jokes and embarrassed local actors trying to earn a quick American buck without anyone noticing.

The buddy duo act (nerdy white guy and jocular, chubby, black offsider) is so relentlessly hackneyed and moronic that the kangaroo easily out-acts the human stars, even though it speaks only once and has just one outfit. Skippy will be turning in his grave.

Delight in the Shite

MORONIC MAFIA
The entire movie hinges on this plot: the boys have ostensibly been sent to Australia to deliver money, but we learn early on that stepdad has arranged for someone to off them when they get there. The $50,000 they're carrying is payment for the hit. We ask: why spend the extra dosh flying the prats to the other side of the world when they could have been dispatched more quickly and easily in a local dark alley?

AUSTRALIA . . . ISN'T THAT IN SCOTLAND?
Known even to the most remedial geography students for its vastness, Australia shrinks to a dinky-Bonsai version in which the outback is a suburb of Sydney, and it takes

a mere morning to traverse the country. Watch the real estate prices soar in remote Coober Pedy as locals see this film and learn they're actually just a 20-minute commute from Sydney Airport.

HOPPING MAD

Check out Louis' jacket on the kangaroo – a perfect fit. This is odd, when you consider that Louis is a great, big, fat bloke ten times the size of your average roo.

ILLEGAL IDIOTS

It's hard to accept that Charlie and Louis' journey would ever have been possible. Considering less than 23 per cent of Americans own passports, the chances of such a couple of criminal dullards having them are slimmer than a kangaroo stealing a large sum of money. Or the father of Liz Hurley's giant baby making a quality movie.

Cite the Shite

'It's the national symbol of Australia – and I've killed it!'
Louis takes out Shane Warne

'I did read the chapter on how an aborigine can kill a white man with a twig. Do you want to see that one?'
Yes!

Make a Shite Night of it

WALKABOUT

Draw a map of Australia according to *Kangaroo Jack*. As this will be a tiny map, try competing to fit your maps onto the smallest surface possible – for example: a cigarette packet or grain of rice.

FOREIGN FUN

Each person assumes the identity of a foreign national for the evening. You may only speak in clichés and behave according to your country's national stereotype. Costume optional.

FEEL THE RUSH

Wear a heart monitor throughout the movie and regularly measure your pulse rate. If it does not race, send your copy of *Kangaroo Jack* to Steve Bing, and demand a settlement for breach of promise.

NEW YORK MINUTE

2004

What they wasted:
$US 30,000,000

Minutes you'll lose:
87

THE GUILTY

Director: **Dennie Gordon**
Jane Ryan: **Ashley Olsen**
Roxy Ryan: **Mary-Kate Olsen**
Max Lomax: **Eugene Levy**
Jim the bike messenger: **Riley Smith**

TRAILER TRASH

It all happens in a New York minute.

The Story

In the absence of talent, you've got to have a gimmick and, luckily for them, the Olsen twins were born with one: they look the same. They also look like the love children of Cameron Diaz and Donald Duck, but we've all got our crosses to bear.

In an America where people who haven't appeared on a television series are now in the minority, being genetic lookey-likeys was enough to ensure the Olsens didn't just become a two-for-one famous face, but a brand.

By the time they were 15, there were marykateandashley videos, books, magazines and a fashion label. As they turned 18, it was time to put the brand on the big screen – which is similar to offering a Big Mac its own action movie, or an iPod a rom-com.

Consequently, anyone who suspected that simply looking like someone else doesn't mean you are gifted was proved right – two Olsens don't make for one good scene, let alone nearly 90 minutes of screwball comedy.

And that's what makes *New York Minute* such a comforting movie to watch – it is both the beginning and the end of the Olsens on the big screen (ever since it sunk like a bag full of ballast, Ashley has devoted herself to business matters, while Mary Kate has concentrated on not eating anything).

It means you can enjoy it, safe in the knowledge that every sight gag, every lame line, every comedy foreigner, every cliché and every stereotype is another nail in the coffin of the terrible twins' movie career.

With a plot in which the bowel movements of a chihuahua are pivotal to the dramatic tension and the most poignant moment occurs in a New York sewer tunnel, every nail that hits home should be accompanied by cheers, champagne and hi-fives with your fellow sufferers.

Rejoice in the fact that you are witnessing the celluloid death of two horrors that may have become *The Sweetest*

Two wrongs don't make a right

*Thing*s (see page 88) of tomorrow if *New York Minute* hadn't garnered a shameful $US5.96 million in its opening weekend, making its box office takings the only truly funny thing about it.

After the euphoria of getting to the final credits without having seen one amusing line or good piece of acting, sit down and write a letter of thanks to the three – count'em, three – screenplay writers who clearly sacrificed their own careers so the Olsens' own would be stopped in its tweeny tracks.

Let's hope to god this trio of pen-pushing heroes are called into action again if Paris and Nicky Hilton ever decide to hook up for a comedy caper.

Delight in the Shite

PERVERT ALERT

While his finer moments include *A Mighty Wind* and *Best in Show*, Eugene Levy also has *Dumb and Dumberer: When Harry Met Lloyd* and *Cheaper By the Dozen 2* to answer for. But none of them compares with his poor decision to play Max Lomax, a truancy inspector who is treading a thin line on the decency front. His obsession with catching serial truant Roxy extends to having his wall covered in photos of her. This isn't a man you'd want following children. Not even the Olsens deserve that.

WHAT ARE THE CHANCES?

Despite New York having 18,976,457 citizens and occupying 141,205 km^2, Jim the bike messenger repeatedly bumps into Jane every time she turns a corner, causing her to perform yet another pratfall with all the comic precision of a buffalo. If only Jim were Jim the van driver and hit her at speed, just once, we all could have been spared the sight of Jane's legs akimbo, sprawled out on a New York sidewalk every 20 minutes.

OH, GROW UP

This was meant to be the twins' coming of age movie, which they clearly felt required them to show more flesh than a Britney Spears video clip. It's mere minutes before Jane's long skirt has been 'accidentally' ripped into a mini skirt. Next they're doing away with clothes altogether and wearing towels in a stranger's hotel room. It's about as sexy as Jack Osbourne in a bikini.

OH, FROCK UP

When they do decide to dress properly again, it is courtesy of a helpful salon owner. To ensure a marykateandashley fashion parade, they try on an endless assortment of outfits before the nice lady allows them to leave her shop looking like two teenage street walkers. Are there no responsible adults in New York?

OXFORD, LONDON

Jane is supposedly a child genius destined to win a scholarship, so how come neither she, nor even the trust that is handing out the prize, knows that Oxford University isn't in London? There's a clue in the name. We're sure the dons of one of England's most hallowed seats of learning would be desperately hoping Jane stays in America, Manhattan.

Cite the Shite

'What are you? A couple of monsters?'
A fellow train passenger touches on the truth

'Right now, that dog is my life. And when he poops, his poop is my life.'
Jane has a rare moment of self-awareness

Make a Shite Night of it

EVIL TWIN

Divide your friends into two teams and get them to prepare an argument about which Olsen twin is the most irritating. The winning side receives a novelty duck.

GOOD TWIN

Have a life-size cardboard cut-out of yourself made, take it with you on job interviews and see if it doubles your earning power. If it doesn't, dress it as a hooker and try again.

THE PRINCE AND ME

2004

What they wasted:
$US 22,000,000

Minutes you'll lose:
111

THE GUILTY

Director: **Martha Coolidge**
Paige Morgan: **Julia Stiles**
Prince Edvard: **Luke Mably**
Soren: **Ben Miller**
Queen Rosalind: **Miranda Richardson**
King: **James Fox**

TRAILER TRASH

The fairytale . . . for real!
Every girl's dream is about to come true . . .

The Story

If this is a modern fairy story, can we have the Grimm brothers back? The child-frightening pair would have struggled to conjure up anything scarier than this tale of a thick-ankled party-pooper and her prince – a lanky eurotrash layabout with an unreliable accent and a fondness for pork products.

The Prince and Me alarmed many social commentators because its heroine sacrifices her independence for a man. This is certainly an outdated message for a 21st century love story, but we find it far more unforgivable that the man in question has less charm than both Cinderella's ugly sisters put together. And he looks like a botched Prince William waxwork left too close to the radiator.

Check out Prince Edvard of Denmark's courtship moves: he introduces himself to his lady by asking her to remove her top; shows off with some explosions in the chemistry lab and, as the ultimate love token, presents her with an industrial meat slicer. Chivalry isn't just dead – it's chopped into little pieces and served up in a Danish cheese and ham sandwich.

Mind you, it's hard to feel sorry for Sir Slice-a-lot's sweetheart when she spends all her spare time sticking pins in a map of places with nasty diseases. Paige, a farm girl from Wisconsin, wants to be a doctor and save the world. This means she can't smile, drink beer or have any fun.

Having shagged all the women in Denmark, the Prat Prince has come to America looking for wild and raunchy college girls. Imagine his disappointment when the first one he meets makes a mother superior look like Madam Whiplash.

Things eventually start to heat up when she teaches him how to use a top-loader washing machine and he recites some *Hamlet*. The pair begin an implausible romance, which plays out against the heady backdrop of a Wisconsin dairy farm and the sort of theme park version of modern Denmark that could only be conceived by Americans without passports.

As the star-crossed lovers grapple with class differences, milk some cows and solve Denmark's workforce problems over the kitchen table, our thoughts turn longingly from the meat slicer to the guillotine.

Delight in the Shite

WE'LL ALWAYS HAVE THE MEAT SLICER

Bewitched by Paige's dishcloth shuffle – displaying a fine pair of cankles – and undeterred when she repels his advances with a high-pressure soda spray, Edvard falls even harder when she pulls on a pair of rubber gloves and shows him her industrial meat slicer. It's like the pottery scene in *Ghost*, except with ham. Later, in the royal palace, Edvard presents his princess with a meat slicer as a token of love and wonders why this makes her cry. Perhaps the Danes can only understand life in terms of bacon.

HOGGING THE LIMELIGHT

Great movie-making's all in the detail. Note the authentic bacon headlines in every Danish newspaper we see. Example: *Pork Industry in Peril!*

TÊTE DU FROMAGE

Look out for the man wearing a cheese on his head in the audience at the country lawnmower race in Paige's home town. Is he a Danish spy, or just an extra making a statement about the movie?

A bichon frise on your head and an American on your back was Denmark's highest honour

PRAT ON PARADE

It's the movie's most touching moment: Paige follows her prince to Denmark and finds him trotting through the Copenhagen streets on horseback in slow motion, with what appears to be a bichon frise stapled to his forehead. You will cry.

Cite the Shite

'I need to get out of Denmark! I need to clear my head!'

When others reach for Panadol, Edvard summons a private jet. How does he treat the flu – with an Apollo shuttle launch?

'Denmark isn't ready for a queen like me.'

Odd, when you consider that it recently settled for a Tasmanian PR girl

'That is the beauty of a meritocracy.'

Kids – did you hear that sociological message?

'Is there a country called Flem?'

No, but it's not a bad movie title

Make a Shite Night of it

PIN THE CHEESE ON THE EXTRA

Everyone wears blindfolds and attempts to attach a piece of real cheese to the foreheads of all the other players. For extra fun, substitute the cheese for a bichon frise.

NAME THAT DANE

Take it in turns to mime a famous Danish person. NB: if there are too many players and not enough famous Danish people, Belgians can be included.

EDVARD'S TOWER OF BABEL

Using Lego, construct a tower by adding a brick each time Edvard's accent changes. The architect of the tallest tower wins a week's supply of bacon.

THE TERMINAL

2004

What they wasted:
$US 60,000,000

Minutes you'll lose:
124

THE GUILTY

Director: **Steven Spielberg**
Viktor: **Tom Hanks**
Amelia: **Catherine Zeta-Jones**
Frank Dixon: **Stanley Tucci**
Gutpa: **Kumar Pallana**

TRAILER TRASH

Life is waiting.

The Story

Meet Viktor: He's Krakozhian, which means he is foreign, which means he can't speak 'American' and that can only mean one thing; he's simpler than Forrest Gump crossbred with *I Am Sam*.

Indeed, so moronic is Viktor that when he turns up in New York's JFK Airport, it seems this isn't just his first trip abroad – it's actually his first time outside his own home.

All of which is an excellent excuse to have him fall over often, use a handful of irrelevant pidgin English punctuated with noises only the Teletubbies could decipher, wear badly knitted jumpers, walk like a bowed-legged bear and – worst of all – be naively sincere.

While all of that should automatically qualify you for an American passport with 'Tom Hanks' written on it, poor Viktor isn't allowed out of the airport, allegedly because Krakozhia ceased to exist during his flight, but mainly because Spielberg has to fit an enormous amount of product placement into just over two hours.

As Hugo Boss, Burger King and every other airport brand linger in each shot, the genius that is Spielberg finally weds Hollywood and mass consumerism together to

'Yeeeeey-es'

produce a whole new genre – shopping channel shite.

As Viktor lumbers his way around what can only be described as a small, contained patch of mall-hell, Spielberg and Hanks try to convince us this is all really a Capraesque fable about the little man triumphing over the big, bureaucratic machine. What we get is a silly foreigner running into plate glass windows, mistaking the ladies' for the men's toilet, saying 'yey-es' to every question he's asked and then, for some mystifying reason, endeavouring to romance an air hostess by building her a mosaic feature wall out of an old urinal.

Terminal? Absolutely – unless you clip in the safety belt, bar all the exits and learn to enjoy this Spielbergian shite.

Delight in the Shite

WHERE IS KRAKOZHIA?
Judging from Viktor's behaviour, Krakozhians are the tribe Europe forgot. Things they don't appear to have include payphones, trolleys (possibly even the wheel), bleepers, phrasebooks, anger and glass. On the other hand, they do have high pants and a happy disposition, so it can't be all bad.

LOVE IS IN THE AIR CON
He may be an idiot but Viktor has an eye for an air hostess with a problematic love life and a penchant for Napoleonic history. He even manages to get Amelia out – well, in – for dinner. The fact she fails to notice it's on an observation deck and the waiter is an Indian minimum wage earner whose idea of a floor show is spinning plates, should mean she's Viktor's perfect match. Sadly, it isn't long before Amelia starts to ask questions (though, naturally, Viktor doesn't understand a single one of them).

TO VIKTOR, THE SPOILS
Let's not write Viktor off. On the one hand, he clearly doesn't understand a word of English. On the other, he manages to teach himself some useful phrases from a book. On the one hand, he appears to have absolutely no idea why he has to stay in the airport. On the other, he can fill out complicated immigration forms (which he chooses to do every day). On the one hand, he gets the chance to leave the airport early. On the other, he's clever enough to realise it's probably

nicer than the rest of America and doesn't bother.

URINAL, I'M WRONG
Love possesses Viktor to strip down a wall of urinals and turn them into a symbol of love, but why does the foreman of the airport renovations not wonder why?

YOU'VE GUTPA LAUGH
In what is meant to be one of the more poignant moments of the movie, cleaner Gutpa tells the story of how he fled India – leaving behind his wife and children – after killing a corrupt policeman. Apparently, he would have got seven years in jail for the crime but, instead, has chosen 30 years in America without his family. Perhaps he can't do maths . . .

Cite the Shite

'You are living at Gate 67; I just want to know why.'
Amelia shows she didn't get to be an air hostess for nothing

'I'm as bad as Napoleon. I just keep ingesting these poisonous men.'
Napoleon might have something to say about that, Amelia

Make a Shite Night of it

VIKTOR SAYS
Go out one night as Viktor but only use his favourite phrases (listed below) and see how far you get:
'Yey-es'
'Yeeeey-es'
'Sensible heels'
'Krakozhia'
'Tuuuu-es-day'

WHAT'S IN THE TIN?
Get each of your guests to bring a peanut tin with something unusual in it (empty the peanuts first), then try to guess What's in the Tin! The winner gets a holiday to Krakozhia.

DINNER PARTY FUN
Invite friends to dinner and then, for no reason, have another friend juggle and spin plates in front of them. Don't refer to it; just carry on having dessert and see if anyone notices.

Naughty Shite

Showgirls (1995)
Striptease (1996)
Swept Away (2002)
The Sweetest Thing (2002)

SHOWGIRLS

1995

What they wasted:
$US 45,000,000

Minutes you'll lose:
128

THE GUILTY

Director: **Paul Verhoeven**
Nomi Malone: **Elizabeth Berkley**
Cristal Connors: **Gina Gershon**
Zack Carey: **Kyle McLachlan**

TRAILER TRASH

Sensual. Controversial. Available.

Beyond your wildest dreams. Beyond your wildest fantasies.

The Story

When Elizabeth Berkley's disturbing face fills the screen in the opening sequence of *Showgirls*, you are witnessing a piece of history. The close-up of this plain, smacked-mouth star with her industrial-strength make-up and hooker's outfit is so much more than the start of a gloriously bad movie. It is nothing less than the birth of shite itself.

Showgirls, brought to you by those connoisseurs of fluff and muff, Paul Verhoeven and Joe Eszterhas, was the first mainstream modern movie to attract audiences just because it was so spectacularly, remorselessly, irredeemably bad. It is the mother of all shite, the progenitor; the egg from which hatched every turkey that has since clucked, gobbled and waddled its way onto the big screen. The influence of *Showgirls* pervades all the movies in this book, sometimes overtly, sometimes subtly – but it is always present. Wherever there is shite, there is *Showgirls*.

Even the makers couldn't pretend it was anything but a ridiculous mishap. While Eszterhas described it as 'disastrous and terrifyingly over the top', Verhoeven commented: 'I think it was bad, too.'

In the beginning, the attempted exposé of Las Vegas loose morals was sold as 'one of the most controversial and shocking films of all time'. But the only shocking part is that it actually made it into cinemas.

Instead of an innocent heroine corrupted by big city sleaze, we have Berkley's Nomi Malone, a girl from the wrong side of the tracks with a burning ambition to be on the even wronger side of the tracks. Her guiding mantras are 'life sucks' and 'shit happens', and if anyone even slightly offends her she flies at them like a rabid Doberman. If it's hard to sympathise with a cussin', stroppy slapper whose ultimate goal is to pop out of a

Nomi waited patiently for the firemen to arrive

fibreglass volcano with no top on, then try some of the other characters: leering, sort-of-lesbian Cristal Connors, who is Vegas' reigning showgirl despite dancing as if fending off an unseen assailant; pest James, who has a self-confessed 'problem with pussy', and Zack, the strip club boss, played with all the personality of a pencil by Kyle McLachlan who, with his bizarre asymmetrical fringe, literally does have one eye on the script. And of course, there are monkeys.

There's an encyclopedia of shite to be filled with quotes from this movie, but the one that says it all most succinctly is uttered by an anonymous stripper in the dressing room: 'upstage left; monkey shit'.

If you can't find *Showgirls* in your DVD store, just follow those directions.

Delight in the Shite

HAND JIVE

The art of top-level exotic dancing appears to consist mainly of fast, complicated hand movements. When Nomi 'burns' on stage, she looks like a deaf person signing a heated argument. Despite this, everyone who witnesses her physical jerks pronounces her a dance genius.

BEWARE! CHARISMA-FREE ZONE

Elizabeth Berkley has one of those faces that makes your mother tut and say sadly: 'poor lass'. Boobs are not enough – even in this film. It cries out to be saved by a stunning, charismatic female lead (Nomi's part was originally written for Sharon Stone), not a star with the screen presence of a welder's bench.

HOW MUCH?

Funny, this: everyone who meets the swearing, scantily clad, over-made-up, violent Nomi on her way into Vegas assumes she's a hooker. She's affronted, although frankly they're being generous.

HANDS OF HELL

It's a buddy scene like you've never witnessed before: two sour-faced exotic dancers bonding over their fondness for snacking on dog food.
Cristal: I've had dog food.
Nomi: You have?
Cristal: Mmm-hmmm. Long time ago. Doggy Chow. I used to love Doggy Chow . . .
Ruff.

WATER SPORT

It has to be the un-sexiest sex scene ever filmed. Nomi, thrashing furiously in a swimming pool, locked on to Kyle McLachlan with her face contorted in an expression of apparent agony, appears to be having a violent seizure or enormous electric shock. It's like watching one of the more gruesome shark attacks in *Jaws* – except without the blood – and a better contraceptive than anything from the chemist. Watch it once and you will never make love again without the grisly spectacle of this writing pair burned onto your retina.

Cite the Shite

'Who wants to see her snatch, anyway?'
What the casting director should have said at Elizabeth Berkley's audition

'I want my nipples to press, but I don't want them to look like they're levitatin'!'
Cristal is a perfectionist

'Polly-Ann Costello. Your father killed your mother and then killed himself.'
Zack reveals Nomi's parents were the lucky ones

'She's no butterfly, Tony, she's all pelvic thrust. I mean, she prowls. She's got it!'
Marty Jacobsen, dance critic

Make a Shite Night of it

DOG'S DINNER

Serve snacks in dog bowls. These might include suspicious-looking stew, bone-shaped biscuits and, for the adventurous, raw chicken wings.

FUNNY MONKEY BUSINESS

Pledge cash to a monkey rescue charity each time Nomi reveals her boobs. During one viewing, you could save several endangered species.

SHOWGIRLS: THE BORED GAME

For a sensual party with a difference, try sexing things up *Showgirls*-style. Throw yourselves to the ground, hurl water, jerk uncontrollably, hit each other and yell. See if anyone falls in love.

STRIPTEASE

1996

What they wasted:
$US 50,000,000

Minutes you'll lose:
117

THE GUILTY

Director: **Andrew Bergman**
Erin Grant: **Demi Moore**
David Dilbeck: **Burt Reynolds**
Darrell Grant: **Robert Patrick**
Shad: **Ving Rhames**
Al Garcia: **Armand Assante**

TRAILER TRASH

Demi Moore at her sexiest.

Some people get into trouble . . . no matter
what they wear.

The Story

When it forced itself upon unsuspecting audiences like a pant-dropping party pest, *Striptease* delivered on just one promise: 'comedy where you least expect to find it.'

This was supposed to mean the movie was satirical, like the novel that inspired it. But when test audiences wept with mirth not at the 'satirical' bits but at everything else, it became clear *Striptease* was in fact a triumph of accidental comedy. And so the makers pretended they'd always intended the whole thing to be hilarious.

Right from the start, everything about *Striptease* should have shouted 'shite'. First, the plot: one young mum's fight to win custody of her daughter when the law doesn't want to know. How does the plucky lady battle an unfair system? Not with protests, letters to her MP or the help of a pressure group, but by pole-dancing in a club called 'The Eager Beaver'. Someone should tell Amnesty International they could beat global injustice if they just put on some crotchless pants and nipple tassels.

Then there's the star. If satire's what you're after, you don't hire Demi Moore, who is to humour what Rob Schneider is to film noir. More power tool than person, with her rigid, shiny surfaces and high-torque thrusting action, Moore thrashes through the stripteases wearing nothing but a snarl and a pair of lawn bowls for breasts. Although her nude appearances were hugely hyped and the entire movie was a vehicle for her abs, these are probably the least erotic naked scenes ever filmed (apart from those in *Showgirls*, see page 76). For the $12 million it cost to hire Moore, they could have borrowed a monkey wrench, put a wig on it and spent the rest on some better plastic surgery for co-star Burt Reynolds, who even in 1996 was starting to resemble a *Thunderbirds* puppet.

But the real magic of *Striptease* lies in the exceptional value it offers to connoisseurs of shite. It contains an entire multiplex of bad cinema, which can only result when six movies collide and get caught between Demi Moore's thighs.

Never mind the same page – no-one's even on the same script. Burt's reprising the madcap hi-jinks of *The Cannonball Run*; Ving

Demi couldn't decide who to shoot first: the director or producer

Delight in the Shite

Rhames is doing *Pulp Fiction*'s deadpan wit; Armand Assante is brooding away in an intense psychological thriller, and shouty Robert Patrick is trapped on *The Jerry Springer Show*. When she's not impersonating a pile driver, Moore is starring in a weepie telemovie, intoning gems such as: 'My husband is addicted to pills and, because of his arrest record, I lost my job as a secretary with the FBI', with moist eyes and wistful gaze.

Until they finally converge in a *Scooby Doo*-style cartoon caper finale, these various planets are visited by a supporting cast of monkeys, boa constrictors, cockroaches and joke breasts. It's the freak show that keeps on giving.

Sit back, enjoy . . . and experience the many faces of shite.

SOMEONE'S GOT TO DO IT

Erin was an FBI secretary and had never stripped in her life. And yet instead of clerical work or even a checkout job, she opted to impress the family court judge with a new career in topless pole-dancing. We never find out where the shy mum learned to pump and grind like a pro and how she came to have the body of the World's Strongest Man.

HAPPY STALKING

Luckily for Erin's persistent stalker, Jerry, she seems to mistake him for a good bra. 'You've always been so supportive of me,' she says, as he pesters her for the umpteenth time.

SEND FOR HUMAN RESOURCES

Erin decides to lobby the 'Eager Beaver' bosses for better strippers' rights. Her main whinge? Not the low wages, humiliating acts, poor conditions and sleazy punters – but the club's rude joke napkins, which are 'really exploitative to women'.

HOITY TOITY

On her high horse once more, Erin blasts Dilbeck: 'Don't ever invade my private life again!' Unfortunately, she's also on the coffee table of his yacht, stripped to her knickers and about to smear him all over with something gooey from the kitchen.

THE *STRIPTEASE* GUIDE TO STRIPPERS

Strippers are terribly misunderstood. Luckily, *Striptease* provides the facts about these plucky professionals, including:

- They've got hearts of gold
- They're smarter and sassier than everyone else
- They're kind to animals – even boa constrictors and incontinent monkeys
- They're always nice to each other
- They're pretty enough to be models
- They once had proper jobs and just had some bad luck
- They have very discerning taste, and won't do dodgy acts with vegetables.

Cite the Shite

'It's good, honest work.'
The strippers welcome Erin to the factory floor

'Dad, there's a floater!'
This little boy sees dead people in his dad's lake

'How'd I get so popular?'
We guess it's all that naked grinding, Demi

'I want to lead a fully dressed life.'
Erin was driven by ambition

Make a Shite Night of it

WHICH BIT'S REAL?

If your guests have been drinking heavily or aren't clever, ask them to count Demi's Moore's fake body parts. For players who prefer a tougher challenge, ask them to spot the real ones.

MONKEY BUSINESS

Leave a monkey alone in a garage, and see how long it takes to construct a Demi Moore. Also leave a typewriter in case it wants to write *Striptease 2*.

SWEPT AWAY

2002

What they wasted:
$US 10,000,000

Minutes you'll lose:
89

THE GUILTY
Director: **Guy Ritchie**
Amber Leighton: **Madonna**
Giuseppe 'Pepe' Esposito: **Adriano Giannini**
Tony Leighton: **Bruce Greenwood**
Marina: **Jeanne Tripplehorn**

TRAILER TRASH
Imagine being shipwrecked on a desert island . . . with someone you really can't stand!

It was about having it all, until it was all . . . swept away!

The Story

Essential viewing for the morbidly curious, this desert-island dog's dinner represents so much more than a triumph of woeful filmmaking. It provides a rare chance to witness the demise of a director's career.

There is little doubt that this remake of an arty Italian movie about a rich bitch (Madonna) stranded on a desert island with a poor, communist deckhand (Giannini) signalled the end of Ritchie's time in the sun.

Opinions differ on which exact *Swept Away* moment sounded the death knell for Mr Madonna. Some believe it was all over as soon as the missus uttered her first line. Others blame the execrable dream sequence, or one of the many toe-curling sado-masochism scenes and implausible plot developments.

One thing is certain: we may never know what made Ritchie, auteur of two successful Brit-gangster movies, hurl himself at this doomed project like a lemming, but the result is a real-life tragedy more compelling even than the shite-fest on screen.

After the 2002 movie was greeted with widespread derision (one reviewer compared it to 'monkeys flinging their faeces at you'), Ritchie took to wearing white and immersed himself in his wife's Kaballah religion. He doesn't get out much anymore.

If you have a heart, you may feel a little sorry for Ritchie; wishing, perhaps, you could have told him that casting his muscle-bound missus was his first – and greatest – mistake. Madonna is as famous for being box office poison as she is for

Slept Away

singing. There is no such thing as a Madonna vehicle – only a Madonna road accident; think *Shanghai Surprise*, *The Next Best Thing* and *Who's That Girl?*

Next, you might have had a word in Ritchie's ear about the wisdom of remaking a socio-politically themed Italian art-house film called *Swept Away by an Unusual Destiny in the Blue Sea of August*, when you're a bloke who makes geezer movies with names like *Snatch*.

Finally, you might have suggested some counselling for a man inexplicably keen to show the world his wife being beaten, humiliated and exploited. More so when you consider that Amber Leighton, Madonna's character, is also Ritchie's mum's maiden name.

Swept Away is shite at its finest, but also provides a poignant reminder that in Hollywood, the line between milestone and gravestone is perilously thin.

Delight in the Shite

BOTOX THOSE BICEPS!

Madonna's arms are *Swept Away*'s hardest working cast members, dominating scenes and (charitably) diverting attention away from the script. They are, simply, huge. Arnie, Vin Diesel, Van Damme huge. If she wasn't wearing a bikini you'd swear Madonna, not Adriano Giannini, was the posh yacht's deckhand – yet she's playing one of those social X-rays who believe you can never be too rich or too thin. So why is she built like a butcher's dog?

LOVE IS A MANY SPLENDOURED THING

Rich girl gets stranded on desert island with poor boy. Before you can say 'prole', poor boy morphs from morose moron into violent psycho. A couple of punches and one attempted rape later, our heroine's in love. Pure Disney.

Without the pantomime acting and vaudeville script ('run, you little vixen, run!') this implausible, misogynous plot would be too distressing to watch. Instead, it makes for great slapstick.

A COMEDY SADIST

Behold the true meaning of knockabout humour. Chortle as Amber snogs Giuseppe's toes. Guffaw as he forces her to sing (it's Madonna, pretending she can't sing – geddit?) and titter as the pair engage in the sort of foreplay David Attenborough might expect to observe in a particularly aggressive insect species.

WHOSE ARM IS IT ANYWAY?

As Amber and Giuseppe cuddle up in bed, one thing remains uncertain: who does the giant, muscular arm in the centre frame belong to?

AS SEEN IN *VOGUE*

Where did Giuseppe get all his soft furnishings? His island tent is flashier than your average city studio apartment. After seeing the pair wash up on the island with only the clothes they were wearing, we must assume someone had pockets big enough for an arty wall-hanging, bed linen and curtains.

Cite the Shite

'I was conceived on the crest of a wave and born in the belly of a boat.'
And, apparently, Giuseppe was educated in a dominatrix dungeon

'Run, you little vixen, run!'
Giuseppe gets all come hither

'I do the jokes around here.'
Giuseppe confesses to writing the script

Make a Shite Night of it

MADONNA'S FACE BINGO

Give each guest a piece of paper with various combinations of Madonna's three facial expressions – pout, grimace and weep – on it. Each time Madonna makes one of these expressions, tick it off your list. First one to tick off all their pouts, grimaces and weeps wins a free pedallo ride at their local boating lake.

SWEPT AWAY CHARADES

Play charades like Amber and Giuseppe; get drunk, make animal noises and jump around.

GIUSEPPE'S JOKES

Nominate your own comedy sadist. Every time Giuseppe biffs Amber, he or she must let off a whoopee cushion, spray everyone with a water pistol or play a Celine Dion CD.

THE SWEETEST THING

2002

What they wasted:
$US 43,000,000

Minutes you'll lose:
88

THE GUILTY

Director: **Roger Kumble**
Christina Walters: **Cameron Diaz**
Courtney Rockcliffe: **Christina Applegate**
Jane Burns: **Selma Blair**
Peter Donahue: **Thomas Jane**

TRAILER TRASH

They're looking for a few good men.

First came the rules of love.
Now comes the fun.

A romantic comedy without the sugar.

The Story

Don't be fooled by the cutesy cover or the sassy *Sex and the City* promises: there is nothing sweet about this tale of three potty-mouthed slappers on a mission to mortify everyone they meet while hunting down a harmless bloke whose only crime was to chat to them in a nightclub.

As soon as Cameron Diaz opens the proceedings with a daft dance along the street for no apparent reason, we wonder: what's wrong with this trio? Their every sentence contains a curse, bowel movement or seminal fluid. They can't balance properly, control their bodily functions or navigate even the simplest social interaction. It's as if you've wandered into a documentary about Tourettes' victims with great hair. Only when everyone else in *The Sweetest Thing* turns out to be equally foul-mouthed do we realise: this is a chick flick gone very, very bad.

The story about three fun-lovin' singletons was clearly inspired by *Sex and the City*'s girl-power success. But instead of jumping on that bandwagon, this film hijacks it then defecates explosively all over it.

A bloke in the director's chair perhaps explains why Diaz, Applegate and Blair are the kind of girls only a spotty

Who let the dogs out?

teenage boy could love: they're bawdy simpletons who like to get laid, dress like hookers and can't stop feeling their own boobs in public.

Only a bloke, and a daft one at that, could sell this as a girl-power movie. Its portrayal of women makes Benny Hill look like Andrea Dworkin's radical disciple. And it's grosser than a septic tank.

In our pursuit of shite, we're practically unshockable (see *Striptease*, page 80 and *Showgirls*, page 76) – but parts of *The Sweetest Thing* actually made us cover our eyes. You can only flinch as the grim burlesque of semen stains, maggots and exploding urinals finally culminates in the unedifying spectacle of Selma Blair impaled by the mouth on her boyfriend's penis while a watching crowd joins with her in singing Aerosmith's *I Don't Wanna Miss a Thing*. This scene lives on in your darkest nightmares like nothing from *The Exorcist* ever could.

Stomach-churning it might be, but *The Sweetest Thing* is essential shite viewing. The transformation of the world's most innocuous genre into an abomination so repugnant it has to be seen to be believed proves that, in Hollywood, anything is possible.

Delight in the Shite

THE PENIS SONG
For once, words completely fail us . . .

You're too big to fit in here (point at crotch),
too big to fit in here (point at mouth),
too big to fit in here (point at bottom)

Your penis packs a wallop,
Your penis brings a load,
And when it makes a delivery
It needs its own zip code

THE SWEETEST THING'S RULES OF FRIENDSHIP:
1 When your friends are depressed, barge into their apartment, rugby tackle them and drag them out to the loudest, brightest and most unpleasant nightclub you can find.
2 Have all your intimate conversations in the toilet, on the toilet or about the toilet.
3 Celebrate your emancipated status by flashing your boobs (especially if they've been enlarged) and bum whenever possible.
4 Be horrible at all times to everyone, including each other.
5 When you run out of swear

words, get wet and writhe around together in your underwear.

6 To bond, call your best girlfriend 'whore', or criticise her intimate hygiene.

7 Fill your life with ice-cream and penises.

THE HUMAN STAIN

Things might have gone better for Clinton if Monica Lewinski had a drycleaner as dedicated as Jane's. When she fronts up the morning after a date with a dress covered in you-know-what, the cleaner tastes it just to make sure.

Cite the Shite

(Caution: these quotes are not for the weak of stomach)

'I can't believe I'm fucking a big purple elephant!'
Neither can we, Jane

'I had lamb curry last night and I'm shitting out a Buick!'
An extra gets the movie's most poetic line

'You cause anal leakage.'
Roger shows guys can talk about emotions too

'Fuck Grandma.'

Grandad proves even passing pensioners can get in on the sewer-talking action

Make a Shite Night of it

WHERE'S THE LOO?

Find a conversation in *The Sweetest Thing* that doesn't contain toilet humour. The first one to succeed wins a plunger.

F&%ଲ$!

While showing the movie, operate a swear box. Put in a coin for every rude word heard on screen and, at the end, spend the proceeds on a yacht or a block of public toilets.

Scary
Shite

Gothika (2004)
Mary Shelley's Frankenstein (1994)
Van Helsing (2004)
Wicker Man (2006)

GOTHIKA

What they wasted:
$US 40,000,000

Minutes you'll lose:
94

THE GUILTY

Directors: **Mathieu Kassovitz** and **Thom Oliphant**
Miranda Grey: **Halle Berry**
Pete Graham: **Robert Downey Jnr**
Sheriff Ryan: **John Carroll Lynch**
Chloe Sava: **Penelope Cruz**

TRAILER TRASH

Because someone is dead doesn't mean
they're gone.

Dr Miranda Grey is an expert at knowing what is
rational, what is logical, what is sane . . . until the
day she woke up on the other side.

The Story

Gothika was made by people who assumed, if they got the name right, everything else would follow – like getting the shoes and hoping the outfit will fall into place. It works better with shoes.

To be fair, the word gothika is a good one – it's a bit like 'gothic', which is a period in history when the rich lived in huge, dark mansions and had their friends made out of old body parts (see *Mary Shelley's Frankenstein* page 98). Plus, gothika has a 'k' in the middle, where you could be forgiven for expecting a 'c' – so it's a clever word to boot.

On the downside, it doesn't really mean anything and is merely a device to make you think 'ooh, horror'. In that sense, it works extremely well.

The first fright is Halle Berry's bad wig, though it's understandable that her psychiatrist doctor, Miranda Grey, might not be taking as much care of her personal appearance as she should. For a start, she's working with Penelope Cruz's looney tune, who would drive anyone to distraction with her indecipherable Spaneth accent.

Secondly no-one ever seems to put enough coins in the electricity meter at the Woodward mental institution, leading to the fluorescent lights constantly flickering. If you weren't insane, you'd definitely become epileptic.

Add to that, the place and everyone in it are clad in so much battleship grey you keep wishing Robert Downey Jnr would turn up in something colourful – like his skin disease from *The Singing Detective* – and you have a working environment even the Wiggles couldn't brighten up.

Strangely none of this bothers Berry, though she does get a little rattled when she wakes up to discover she's now one of the patients, having apparently butchered her husband, no small feat considering he's roughly 23 times her size.

Now all that's left for Miranda is to run up and down badly lit corridors, bang her hands against cell walls, shouting in a deranged way about how not crazy she is, struggle with her wig getting increasingly skew-whiff, and listen to Cruz say things like 'hah con hugh trist some-a-bidy who thinks u rrrrrrrr craz-ee?' What?

To pass the time more quickly, we suggest Berry try to count the horror movie clichés conveniently gathered under the heading *Gothika*. It's a one-stop schlock shop!

Delight in the Shite

CLICHÉ-IKA

Welcome to the encyclopedia of hackneyed horror:

• It's constantly raining and the sun never seems to rise. No wonder people are insane
• The asylum's only colour scheme is grey or, for a change, dark grey
• The generator is constantly failing and cannot be fixed by any engineer
• The girl standing in the road who Berry runs over has standard–issue, Cousin It hair
• Things are played backwards, like Berry's dream, because everyone knows backwards

Berry wasn't possessed, she was deluded

things are frightening
• The basement of the asylum has rats – surely the department of health would be onto this in a public health facility?
• The ghost is an angry teenager who wants our heroine to avenge her murder. Her method for communicating this is by constantly beating Berry half to death – adolescents are obviously obnoxious on both sides of the wall
• There's a bath scene (a) to make sure Berry shows some flesh and (b) because there's always a bath scene
• The friendly asylum security guard is, as always, tubby
• Berry sees a face in her rear-view mirror – what kind of fool would even look?
• The villain has tattoos
• The asylum nurse is strangely sinister, which is odd for someone who has entered the caring profession
• The ghost tries to communicate by breathing on glass and then writing on it – if they've got the ability to return from the dead, why can't they just pass you a note?
• Downey Jnr plays the highly regarded genius psychiatrist who always fails to believe the heroine, even when bloody writing is appearing spontaneously on her skin

before his very eyes. What did he think it was, a shaving accident?

• An owl in the barn Berry is drawn to suddenly swoops down and gives her a fright

• The other mental patients are – bar Cruz who isn't really mental anyway – all ugly and misshapen because good-looking people under size 14 never suffer mental health issues

• When we do see a day scene, a group of catatonic patients are playing volleyball – which isn't a horror movie cliché, but should be.

Cite the Shite

'He opened me up like a flower of pain.'

Chloe proves being crazy doesn't mean you can't use a metaphor

'I'm not deluded, Pete, I'm possessed.'

Miranda's simple explanation

'This isn't logical.'

Was the good Sheriff driven mad by too many *Star Trek* episodes as a child?

Make a Shite Night of it

LIGHTY-LIGHT

Invite your friends round and keep turning the lights on and off. See how long it takes for one of them to take an axe to you.

PLAY INVESTIGATOR

Sheriff Ryan says 'Have you any idea what happens to a small town sheriff when the FBI takes over?' Call FBI headquarters on Pennsylvania Ave, Washington and ask them. To maintain the mystique, tell no-one their answer.

MAD PEOPLE VOLLEYBALL

Take one ball, a net and some friends. Keep throwing the ball at the net without anyone getting it over. It will drive everyone mad.

MARY SHELLEY'S FRANKENSTEIN

1994

What they wasted:
$US 10,000,000

Minutes you'll lose:
119

THE GUILTY

Director: **Kenneth Branagh**
Dr Victor Frankenstein: **Kenneth Branagh**
The Creature: **Robert De Niro**
Elizabeth: **Helena Bonham Carter**

TRAILER TRASH

It's alive!
Be warned.

The Story

From the moment Kenneth Branagh appears as a dot in the distance of some frozen wastes, dragging what looks like a Hills Hoist with him, this has all the hallmarks of being monster shite.

Pulled onboard Aidan Quinn's stranded ship, Ken explains that, no, he isn't taking in washing, but is in fact the infamous Dr Victor Frankenstein . . .

Cue the unfolding of the familiar yarn told with a delicious helping of ham, courtesy of England's greatest luvvie, who sets out to make a movie in which everything is as overblown as his ego.

And so young Frankenstein's mother can't just quietly die in childbirth – we have to see her legs akimbo having a child ripped out of her by her doctor husband displaying all the medical expertise of a blind butcher with no thumbs.

The family house can't just be a mansion; it has to be so cavernous that the Frankensteins can't ever seem to fill it. If Victor really wanted to have been a help, he should have taken up carpentry and made some chairs.

The gay young Alp dwellers of the Frankenstein household can't just go strolling in the

The aerobics lesson was not going well

mountains, they have to lie on the top of the highest peak and try to conduct electricity.

Victor can't just decide to make a new human being out of cadavers; he has to do it in an attic bigger than an aircraft hangar, with huge vats of amniotic fluid and a mystifying pulley system; the sole purpose of which is to provide symbolic chains.

Worst of all, the thin-lipped thespian can't do all of this fully clothed. Instead he constantly bears his chest, despite being in Salzburg, a town not known for its clement weather.

The result of it all is a bacchanalian feast of a movie, a large mirror in which Branagh can stare endlessly at himself and his own pectorals against backdrops that, despite their size, are simply not big enough to contain his huge head. Frankenstein did, indeed, create a monster.

Delight in the Shite

CREATURE DISCOMFORT

Why does De Niro's Creature feel so sorry for himself? After all, Mickey Rourke doesn't let this kind of bad plastic surgery get him down. We're confused, too, by Victor's surprise when the man he's made out of old parts of dead people turns out not to be much of a looker.

DON'T FANCY YOURS MUCH

At the end of the day, all the poor ugly Creature wants is a date – if he wanted something to love him, he'd be better off with a dog. Then again, he eventually does get a dog when Victor creates another sewing disaster and stitches Helena Bonham Carter onto half of another woman, apparently using a fish hook. Quite why they are fighting over this patchwork quilt of a woman is mystifying.

SLIPPERY WHEN WET

How much amniotic fluid can one man gather? The good women of Salzburg must have been terrified of their waters breaking, knowing that Branagh's shady Victor would be along in a jiffy with his bucket. Luckily he gets a vat-full, giving him a good excuse to have the pointlessly long 'birthing' scene, as he and De Niro slippy-slide around like two grown men in a jelly-wrestling competition.

MINISTRY OF SILLY TEETH

John Cleese was obviously so keen to join Branagh's band of luvvies he agreed to suffer for his art and wear a pair of false teeth, apparently borrowed from a horse.

CAN YOU DIRECT ME TO THE SEA OF ICE PLEASE

When the Creature demands a meeting with Victor, he tells him he will rendezvous with him on a sea of ice. Despite these rather vague directions, they manage to find one another, which is lucky because then the Creature gets to push Victor down what appears to be a toboggan run.

Cite the Shite

'The town's people have gone mad!'

Heck! The town's people are always going mad

'Who are these people of which I am comprised?'

The Creature realises he wasn't brought by the stork

Make a Shite Night of it

HAIR TODAY

Using anything you can find around the house – carpet, mops, wood, electrical wire – try to construct Helena Bonham Carter's hair. For bonus points, reanimate it using an electric whisk.

TEAM THOMPSON

Try to spot the moment Branagh decided to leave Emma Thompson for Helena Bonham Carter. Once you've identified it, boo loudly.

VAN HELSING

What they wasted:
$US 160,000,000

Minutes you'll lose:
132

THE GUILTY

Director: **Stephen Sommers**
Van Helsing: **Hugh Jackman**
Anna Valerius: **Kate Beckinsale**
Friar Carl: **David Wenham**
Dracula: **Richard Roxburgh**

TRAILER TRASH

Adventure lives forever.

The one name they all fear.

The Story

Some movies are just plain greedy, and *Van Helsing* is the greediest of them all. Not content with Dracula's yarn, it adds the werewolf legend, throws in Frankenstein, gives a cheeky nod to 007 and a passing hello to both Jekyll and Hyde. It's this kind of rapaciousness that makes us admire *Van Helsing* not only as shite, but thieving shite.

Add to this the fact that none of the classic novels plundered by director Stephen Sommers is treated to anything other than heavy-handed special effects and a script penned by Frankenstein's monster's less articulate brother, and you get a true bout of the gothic horrors.

Perhaps most telling, however, is that one of the only characters created solely for this movie is utterly implausible. It is easier to believe in wolfmen, immortal bloodsuckers and men made out of miscellaneous cadavers than Kate Beckinsale's Anna Valerius.

If it wasn't enough that Beckinsale doesn't really cut it as an action heroine – in the same way, say, Dracula wouldn't cut it as a vegan – Valerius is the worst vampire-hunter ever.

Despite having lost generations of her family to the fang, Princess Anna's vampiric knowledge is poor; she gasps to discover Dracula hasn't got a mirror image and seems amazed he has no heartbeat. Faced with a werewolf in the house, she grabs what looks like a toasting fork. Oh, and worst of all, she runs like a girl. If she's a true representation of the Valerius gene pool, we're siding with the vampires.

Delight in the Shite

IT'S NO TIME FOR KNITWEAR

Poor Van Helsing; not only must he struggle with a useless heroine and an annoying sidekick, but he has to literally wear the indignity of being the worst-dressed slayer in history. Sporting a floppy hat and cumbersome grey cable-knit poloneck, you can only thank heaven he's not pitched against Dracula in a fashion-off – Roxburgh's camp fang-ster would win hands down (despite a cheap, girlie hair ornament or two).

When air kissing goes bad

A NATION OF CURTAIN TWITCHERS

Having lived for hundreds of years in fear of having the blood sucked out of you by a passing vampire, in the knowledge the surrounding woods are teeming with werewolves and who knows what else, you might think Transylvanians would be a naturally cautious race. But no, the minute they hear a rumpus they are out on the street looking at the sky with big 'eat me' signs over their heads. Curiosity not only kills the village cat, but the baker, his wife, the blacksmith and the woman who takes in the washing.

ANNA IN THE SKY WITH DIAMONDS

Surely the most frightening part of the movie is the appearance of a dead Anna, smiling down benignly at a distraught Van Helsing – who is presumably upset at the thought he will never get away from her if she has the power to materialise into cumulus from beyond the grave. No wonder the monster takes his chances on a floating door in the open ocean.

Cite the Shite

'All I wanted was life, Gabriel. The continuation of my kind.'

A broody Dracula has forgotten he's immortal and doesn't need kids

'If there is one thing I've learned, it's never to stick your hand in a viscous material.'

Friar school was thorough in those days

Make a Shite Night of it

LITTLE HUGH RIDING HOOD

Hold a howl-a-thon and campaign heavily to find Hugh Jackman a big-screen role in which he doesn't have to either be a wolf, or be chased by a wolf.

KNIT YOURSELF A HERO

With friends, watch the movie while, at the same time, knitting yourselves superhero jumpers. Whoever has dropped the least stitches by the time Anna appears in the sky, wins a Fedora.

WICKER MAN

2006

What they wasted:
$US 40,000,000

Minutes you'll lose:
115

THE GUILTY
Director: **Neil LaBute**
Edward Malus: **Nicolas Cage**
Sister Summersisle: **Ellen Burstyn**
Willow Woodward: **Kate Beahan**

TRAILER TRASH
Some sacrifices must be made.

The Story

If the director and star of this remake love the 1973 original as much as they've both claimed, they have a very funny way of showing it.

Their 2006 *Wicker Man* is so stupendously shite it was greeted by calls for LaBute and Cage themselves to be burned, like the movie's main character, for their sins against celluloid.

Rarely has a movie attracted such deafening derision. On its release, reviewers hailed it as: 'spectacularly rotten', 'genuinely idiotic', 'a calamity from start to finish', and 'a stupid, stupid movie'. And those are the kinder comments.

Warning bells had sounded early for this doomed fiasco.

There were no press previews and Robin Hardy, the original version's director, instructed his lawyers to remove his name from all promotional material, even before filming was finished. It seemed everyone wanted to wash their hands of whatever monster had been created, and soon it was clear why.

Somehow, a respected cult film had resurfaced as pure pantomime. Piece by piece, the spooky chiller about pagans and human sacrifice had been dismantled and rebuilt as a monument to unintentional farce. In fact, the world's most side-splitting comedians can only dream of being as funny as *Wicker Man's* final scene: Nicholas Cage lumbering around in a bear suit chased

In cod they trust

by women wearing beaks, fish heads and bumblebee outfits led by Ellen Burstyn in a nightie with her face painted blue. The only frightening part of what's meant to be a terrifying climax is that everyone involved managed to keep a straight face.

Cage (his thinning thatch covered with borrowed hair) plays a cop who finds himself in a weird village and quickly sets about being its idiot. This is no mean feat, as all Summersisle's other residents are hatchet-faced women with a fondness for hauling around writhing sacks and speaking in riddles. 'We're different here', they tell Edward. After witnessing their Quaker-chic wardrobe, mute men and the strange contents of their pickle jars, most visitors would assume they had happened upon a Country Women's Association gone very, very bad – then run like crazy.

Everything – from the abundance of scary twins, to the women's botanical names, to the dodgy tale of a missing child who lured him there – screams 'you're going to burn in a big straw man'. But Edward just doesn't see it coming; not when he learns that the schoolgirls' favourite game is trapping birds in their desks 'to see how long they

will last', or that instead of times tables they chant: 'Phallic symbol! Phallic symbol!'; not even when the island's entire population comes after him in bird, fish and deer costumes like a bunch of demented Disney characters.

After lots of shouting and a toupee-off with Queen Bee Ellen Burstyn, Edward hurtles towards his comedy demise and we can only look on in disbelief, shaking not with fear, but mirth.

Delight in the Shite

STICKY

Despite its proximity to the densely populated Washington State coast, Summersisle has no shops and only one source of income: honey. When the bees fail to produce, things look grim for the ladies. Their solution? Send out the only two pretty ones to comb the country for nice blokes to lure back years later as human sacrifices. It's never clear why they didn't just turn their hand to jams and chutneys.

BUZZ OFF

It's soon obvious why the bees on Summersisle aren't making

honey – they're too busy. Their jobs include: being worn as beards by the local ladies; inspiring fancy dress costumes for ritual sacrifices; monstering Edward – who has a convenient bee allergy – and providing clumsy 'drone' and 'Queen Bee' metaphors for those too daft to notice the place is a mentalists' matriarchy.

HE DIED PEACEFULLY

Edward's final moments are meant to be so gory we only hear his dying sounds off-camera and his heart-rending, chilling last call as the nutters of Summersisle fall upon him: 'Argh! Me legs!' (Suggested alternatives: 'Is my hair on straight?' and 'Where's my pussy?')

Cite the Shite

'This here is mead. It's one of the pleasures of our island.'
Sister Beech neglects to mention the women also get their kicks pickling foetuses, wearing animal costumes and training attack bees

'Killing me won't bring back your goddam honey!'
But it will give us another laugh, Edward

'Something bad is about to happen.'
Edward nails the movie's promotional tagline

Make a Shite Night of it

A SLICKER WICKER

Achieve critical acclaim by making your own version of *Wicker Man*, about a day in the life of a cane armchair and its friends. It is guaranteed to be better than this one, thus convincing everyone that you are very clever.

ANIMAL ANTICS

Find someone you don't like, force them to wear a bear, rabbit or deer costume, chase them around town and then kill them violently. If you particularly dislike the person, commute their death sentence to a viewing of *Wicker Man*.

CAGED BEAST

Stand in the middle of a busy shopping mall wearing a bear suit, shout: 'Argh! Me legs!' and see if anyone offers to help.

BAD DATE

Rid yourself of unwanted suitors by enjoying this movie together.

Serious Shite

BIRTH

2004

What they wasted:
$US 20,000,000

Minutes you'll lose:
100

THE GUILTY

Director: **Jonathan Glazer**
Anna: **Nicole Kidman**
Young Sean: **Cameron Bright**
Joseph: **Danny Huston**
Eleanor: **Lauren Bacall**
Clara: **Anne Heche**

TRAILER TRASH

A haunting thriller that will keep you
guessing until the very end.

Be careful what you wish for.

The Story

It's a man in the body of a boy! It's everlasting love! It's a lady who looks like an elf! Sounds like we're in for some wacky hi-jinks from the land of magical make-believe! Or maybe not.

One of the funniest things about *Birth* (and there are many) is how easily this deranged absurdity could have been a feel-good movie in the style of *Big* or *Freaky Friday*.

With CGI, some catchy tunes, a few cute characters or even just some fish that can speak, we might have had a McDonald's kiddie meal in the making.

Instead we get a crazy creep-fest that makes us cover our eyes and cry 'Nooooo!' as it blunders past the 'wrong way, go back' signs towards the outer limits of bad taste.

The opening sequence sets the mood: a man, Sean, jogs for what seems like hours through a park and then suddenly drops dead. We soon realise he was the lucky one.

Ten years later, the deceased Sean's wife Anna (Nicole Kidman, wearing the shorn hairdo of movie widows who hear from their dead husbands) is sought out by a kid claiming to be Sean. Despite his resemblance to Damian's spookier brother and his unconvincing evidence, she believes him.

After this, we can only marvel at the story's demented trajectory. While most parents would march such a boy straight to the child psychologist or at least distract him with a PlayStation, little Sean's folks send him to stay with Anna and her grim family.

This fun-dodging clan consider gloom their higher calling; they don't own a single colour between them, and for kicks they sit stony-faced through Wagner operas or hire string quartets to play dirges in the drawing room.

During this sojourn the ten-year-old takes a sexually charged bath with 30-something Anna, is spanked by her fiancé and verbally abused by her witchy mother. Mum and dad might as well have dispatched him straight to Michael Jackson's Neverland.

What happens? We will only give away this much: if you've ever thought your love life was complex, try Anna's. The dead-hubby-in-a-boy's-body is only the start. Every time you think *Birth* can't get any madder, it cranks up the loon-o-meter just a little bit more.

What we love most about this

'Tom . . . ?'

movie is that everything in it — no matter how barmy or unbelievable — is treated with a po-faced pretentiousness that disappears so far up its own fundament, it's a wonder there's anything left to see. A triumph of style over sanity, *Birth* is priceless viewing for fans of arthouse shite.

Delight in the Shite

DOING A DEMI
Never mind the child; we need counselling after watching him hop into a tub with a woman old enough to be his mother, then talk about how he might 'satisfy her needs'. Our advice to Anna: tell the kid to come back in eight years' time. If he's still keen, she can do a Demi Moore – perfectly acceptable these days.

NICE DAY FOR A SHITE WEDDING
The ordeal is over, Anna and Joseph are tying the knot, and the wedding is . . . a wrist-slitting misery-fest. It takes place on an ugly piece of scrubland and ends with the desolate-eyed bride doing a deranged dance alone on a bleak beach. We can only be thankful we didn't have to witness one of their family funerals.

WHY THE LONG FACE?
At the opera, we're treated to a close-up of Nicole which goes on, and on . . . and on for exactly one minute and 57 seconds. During this time, not a single emotion is visible on her immobile features. Even in fast forward, there is barely a trace of life. At least it provides an ideal time to visit the bathroom or find a stick to poke your eyes out with.

BIRTH – THE MUSICAL
With just a few tweaks, this movie really could have been a jolly, sing-a-long blockbuster (see table).

Birth	Birth, the Musical
A boy comes up with the best line to get out of homework since 'the dog ate it' by claiming he must spend all his time with his wife as he is the reincarnation of her dead spouse. Misery ensues.	A cheating husband makes a wish that he was young again and wakes up as a ten-year-old! As he learns what really counts, can he convince his ex-wife to help her in time to stop her marrying someone else? Hair-raising frolics ensue.
Set in: Gloomy, chilly drawing rooms	Set in: Toontown
Directed by: Jonathan Glazer Starring: Nicole Kidman Cameron Bright Lauren Bacall	Directed by: Baz Luhrmann Starring: Jennifer Lopez Justin Timberlake Angela Lansbury
Score by: Richard Wagner Hit single: Die Walküre: Erster Aufzug	Score by: Elton John Hit single: 'Can You Fill the Bath Tonight?'

Cite the Shite

'I thought you were my dead husband but you're just a little boy in my bathtub.'
Anna wises up

'Is Mr Reincarnation enjoying his cake?'
Sean has trouble with the mother-in-law

Make a Shite Night of it

OSCAR GLORY

She's donned the ugly nose and the horrid wig – but what else could Nicole wear to win an Oscar: A prosthetic hunchback? A goiter? Mail all suggestions to Nicole's American agent.

AGAINST THE CLOCK

See if you can hold your breath for the entire one-minute-57-second close-up of Nicole. Smokers or asthmatics may prefer to see how many tequila shots they can drink during that time.

EYES WIDE SHUT

What they wasted:
$US 65,000,000

Minutes you'll lose:
153

THE GUILTY

Director: **Stanley Kubrick**
Bill Harford: **Tom Cruise**
Alice Harford: **Nicole Kidman**
Victor Ziegler: **Sydney Pollack**
Nick Nightingale: **Todd Field**

TRAILER TRASH

Cruise. Kidman. Kubrick.

The Story

The excitement surrounding *Eyes Wide Shut* back in 1999 is hard to imagine now we've seen Tom jump up and down on Oprah's sofa and Nic win an Oscar for wearing a wax nose.

But back then the combo of the golden couple and Kubrick, the man who gave us *Dr Strangelove* and *2001: A Space Odyssey*, had critics all a quiver with gleeful anticipation.

Perhaps because their expectations had run so high thanks to a painful two-year production that was wrapped in more secrecy than the Enigma code, reviewers everywhere seemed to take leave of their senses when the movie was finally released.

Accolades such as 'masterpiece' were bandied about while the awful truth – that *Eyes Wide Shut* is a real Emperor's New Clothes of a movie or, more accurately, an Emperor's No Clothes – went unnoticed.

Well, not quite. The public spotted the sublime pointlessness of it all straightaway. Where critics saw a dreamlike exploration of sexual obsession, people who actually paid good money to see the 'masterpiece' saw a dull examination of the world's most tedious marriage.

How right they were. In a nutshell; Alice (Kidman) tells hubby Bill (Cruise) she once thought of having a roll in the hay with another bloke. Instead of going out and getting stonking drunk like any normal man, a sulky Bill embarks upon a night-time odyssey in which he completely fails to get a shag. Even at an orgy.

If you can endure it *Eyes Wide Shut* is a marathon of pretentious shite. From the opening scene of our Nic on the loo to the crass final line, it's a ponderous yarn of a woman who's done nothing, a man who can't do anything and the devastation being such almighty bores visits upon their marriage. Masterpiece indeed, though not quite as Kubrick intended.

Delight in the Shite

UN-AUSTRALIAN

It should be a matter of national shame that Kidman's Alice just can't seem to handle either her booze or her pot. At the party, she's a half-glass screamer, falling into the arms of a Latin lothario at the mere whiff of a champagne bubble. Later, she gets extraordinarily stoned after one drag of dope. Worst of all, neither the drink nor the spliff make her any more interesting.

DOCTOR IN THE HOUSE?
We're not sure Bill is qualified as a doctor at all. When he's called upon to help the overdosed hooker at Sydney Pollack's lavish party, he shouts at her, slaps her and then looks in her mouth – all the doctor-type things you might do if you were merely pretending to be a doctor. We're surprised he doesn't check her reflexes with a small hammer and ask her to say, 'Ahhhhhhhhhhh'.

TIS A PITY HE'S A BORE
Among the many questions surrounding the orgy is: why are all these rich people even bothering? Is this what happens when freemasons get frisky? Despite the fact they aren't doing anything illegal, they insist upon using passwords and wearing masks as Cruise stalks around like Phantom of the Orgy, shocked – despite being a doctor (allegedly) – by the listless assortment of middle-aged nude men doing rude things to uninterested girls.

WHEN SCRIPTS RUN OUT
Eyes Wide Shut has to have one of the most groan-worthy endings in the history of groaning. As they are sloping around a store looking like the ghosts of Christmas past, Alice chirps up 'There's something very important we need to do as soon as possible.' 'What?' wonders Bill, perhaps hoping for a visit to Santa's grotto. 'Fuck,' says Alice. It's just not nice talk in a toy department.

ANY REQUESTS?
Why couldn't Bill be a bit more like Nick Nightingale (Todd Field), his piano-playing friend? Nick is a cool barfly who wouldn't bat an eye if he was asked to play 'Everything's Coming Up Roses' at the annual Sodom and Gomorrah summer solstice bash. Now that's entertainment.

Cite the Shite

'As soon as you were gone . . . I felt wonderful.'
Alice to Bill – we know exactly how she felt

'Life goes on, it always does, until it doesn't.'
Pollack's Victor has been doing

too much of that thunking business

Make a Shite Night of it

THE 'AVE YOU EVAH? GAME

Sleazy Hungarian Sandor Szavost asks Alice: 'Did you ever read the Latin poet Ovid on the art of love?' Whenever you go out to a party, use the line to chat someone up and see how successful you are. If it doesn't work, try: 'Did you ever read the later poet Arthur on the yacht of love?', which is what it actually sounds like in Sandor's joke accent.

PAPIER-MÂCHÉ ORGY

Collect old news clippings about Tom and Nicole, and then use them to make papier-mâché. Invite your friends round and try to fashion Tom and Nic masks for everyone. Wear them with nothing else, if that's what floats your boat. Note: only try this at home.

THE HORROR, THE HORROR

When Alice wakes from her nightmare, pause the DVD and take it in turns to guess what it was about. Suggestions such as she dreamed she'd woken up one day and was a scientologist, or she had a vision of hearing endless country music, are totally allowed.

Close your eyes and think of Kubrick

LADDER 49

What they wasted:
$US 60,000,000

Minutes you'll lose:
110

THE GUILTY

Director: **Jay Russell**
Jack Morrison: **Joaquin Phoenix**
Mike Kennedy: **John Travolta**
Linda Morrison: **Jacinta Barrett**
Ray: **Balthazar Getty**

TRAILER TRASH

A bond forged by fire is never broken.

Their greatest challenge lies in rescuing one of
their own . . .

The Story

Contrary to popular opinion, your life doesn't flash before your eyes in seconds as you face impending doom – it takes around two hours and 20 minutes. At least it does for Phoenix's Jack Morrison who, faced with imminent death, chooses to spend his last moments on earth fondly remembering such things as John Travolta and geese.

Made as a heavy-handed tribute to firemen two years after 9/11, *Ladder 49* is the cinematic equivalent to smoking in bed: a silly, potentially damaging choice accompanied by the risk of falling asleep.

The damage here is to the reputation of firemen everywhere. These normally unassailable heroes only come across as being brave because they are dummies who understand nothing about fires but a lot about locker-room pranks. Indeed, if the men of *Ladder 49* weren't firefighters, they would be circus clowns or warm-up acts for bad comics.

If you are unlucky enough to be a rookie, fire chief Travolta likes nothing more than to greet you with his pants off and then insist you make a confession to a passing priest who turns out to be – ha! – not a priest at all.

If you aren't feeling fully bonded to the other men on your watch by this stage, wait until you find a live goose in your locker or the 'old ones are the best' bucket of water over the door. That's bound to make you secure in the abilities of your colleagues as you head out to a towering inferno.

What with practical jokes around every corner, it's amazing Morrison's nerves aren't shot to pieces *before* he starts running into burning buildings – for all he knows, every blaze is just another elaborate jolly jape.

No doubt real fires who are facing danger every day like to let rip with a few laughs every now and then, but the men of *Ladder 49* only seem to have a handful of jokes to play – given

Buffing the pole was such a chore

they spend so much time sitting around, you'd think they'd come up with some new 'get the rookie' scams. Perhaps the electric shock handshake, or the fake dog's turd or the classic 'nail through the finger'. These people just aren't funny.

Jokes aside . . . well, you can't really put the jokes aside for *Ladder 49*, because that's pretty much all there is, bar a line up of All-American hero-types who don't seem to have much going on underneath the fire hat. If only the goose had more scenes.

Delight in the Shite

BOG SNOG
The morning after a heavy night out, Linda and Jack share a romantic snog. Time and time again we see it in movies – after a hard night's drinking, when mere mortals would have breath like a vulture's crotch, the inside of a mouth that feels like a fire hose and a hankering to go hug the toilet, people in movies are still gagging for it – anyone else would just be gagging.

MARRIED TO THE MOB
From the moment Linda is initiated into the gang with some hardcore drinking games, she and Jack rarely enjoy a minute alone. No matter what the occasion, the assorted bunch of misfits who are Jack's workmates are there – from Linda's first phone call to her new boyfriend, to her announcing that she's pregnant. It's amazing they weren't all gathered around the stirrups during the birth, cheering her on, unleashing geese, whooping and cracking inappropriate gags.

BAD MANNERS
Jack may well be a have-a-go hero, but his table manners are those of a starving stray dog. When he and Linda are discussing whether he should take a desk job, Jack conducts the argument with a full mouth of food as he shovels his dinner, one handed, down the hatch. For the unfortunate viewer, it's like staring into a waste disposal chute.

DIDDUMS
Why does Joaquin always look as though he is going to cry? Even during the most mundane scenes he appears to be fighting back the emotion, tears welling, chin quivering. Maybe it's because he already knows the ending or he knows what happened to the goose.

EXTRA! EXTRA!

In a movie like this you have to search long and hard for talent, but we found it in the St Patrick's Day crowd scene, where there's a shaved Shih tzu on a skateboard who's right up there with the cheese-headed extra in *The Prince and Me* (see page 66). The Shih tzu is neither a native animal of Ireland, a natural skateboarder, nor – to our knowledge -– a capable firefighter, but that doesn't stop the camera giving the little fella a tracking shot all of his own.

Cite the Shite

'I keep having that dream about the red car turning up in front of the house when you don't come home.'
Linda's been watching too much Wiggles

'Fire? No. I have a goose in my locker though.'
Another hard day at the fire house for Jack

'You get in enough fires, you find God.'
Ray's approach to religion is riskier than most

Make a Shite Night of it

WILD GOOSE CHASE

Obtain a goose by whatever means necessary and place it in a friend's cupboard or wardrobe when they're not looking. When they stop finding it funny, set fire to their house.

COUNTDOWN

Count the number of appalling, soft rock songs that mark pivotal moments of Morrison's life. It must have been a relief to not pull through if all you've got to look forward to is being followed around by third rate rocker Robbie Robertson whining a dirge called 'Shine a Light' like Jon Bon Jovi at a karaoke bar. See if you can come up with a worse 'life soundtrack' for yourself.

NAUGHTY

Play with matches. Because you shouldn't.

PAPARAZZI

What they wasted:
$US 20,000,000

Minutes you'll lose:
81

THE GUILTY

Director: **Paul Abascal**
Bo Laramie: **Cole Hauser**
Detective Burton: **Dennis Farina**
Wendell Stokes: **Daniel Baldwin**
Leonard Clark: **Tom Hollander**
Rex Harper: **Tom Sizemore**

TRAILER TRASH

They were after a story. Now, he's after them.

One good shot deserves another.

The Story

Movie stardom, it's a trial. Take poor Bo Laramie (Hauser), a simple Montana family man who is so astonishingly naïve he's surprised when his search for fame leads to being famous. Bo is so fresh off the farm that he's apparently new to the planet. Why, he wonders, can't he be famous without retaining his anonymity?

Imagine his discomfort then when, whilst minding his own business walking down the red carpet to the opening of his movie, there are people there with little machines that flash at you. Bo feels violated – this kind of thing never happened in Montana.

There's worse to come for our flannel-shirted hero; soon Bo is the quarry of a fringe-dwelling paparazzi gang consisting of ex-rapists, fraudsters and random nutters.

Thus begins producer Mel Gibson's indulgent poison pen letter to all the members of the media who have selfishly helped make him one of the most powerful men in Hollywood. Thank God he let his ex-hairdresser direct it, or *Paparazzi* might have actually made a point rather than being the movie equivalent to a bad perm – a lifeless thing you'd rather forget.

Far from being a meditation on the privacy/fame trade-off, the depth of Bo's soul-searching is bludgeoning a snapper to death. Wouldn't it be easier to hire a bodyguard and good publicist?

Tom Sizemore, Daniel Baldwin and Tom Hollander's paparazzi, meanwhile, are portrayed as so sub-human that – even when clinging by fingertips to a cliff – they choose to sprout a few smart alec barbs rather than accept Bo's offer of life-saving help.

It's this kind of pathological dedication to being complete bastards that makes you start rooting for the paparazzi.

There's nothing we dislike more than celebrities whinging on about wanting to lead normal lives – go on and lead them and stop forcing your faces onto screens everywhere in shite movies; like this one, for instance.

Delight in the Shite

CAST OFFS

Enjoy a fine example of 'ironic' casting; paparazzi basher Baldwin as a mad-eyed voyeur, real life police line-up regular Sizemore as the inexplicably insane Rex and even Gibson himself turning up in the waiting room outside Bo's anger management counselling. If only Mel hadn't missed so many sessions . . .

THE PAPARAZZI FROM HELL

How purely evil are the snappers? Let's recap: they go through garbage, rape girls, make sex videos, have abusive answer machine messages, force Bo to have a car accident and delay calling the ambulance, trick him into a lawsuit, live in houses apparently decorated by the Manson family and the best thing they've got to wear is a permanent sneer. Butterflies everywhere should fear for the safety of their wings.

THE OLD ONES ARE THE BEST

When faced with a movie that's as emotionally engaging as an iron filing, makers of shite everywhere know that the last thing you want to do is add characterisation, a challenging script and exciting direction. Instead find the cutest child actor you can, pop them in a hospital bed in a coma with a plaster on their forehead and have 'mommy' keep a 24-hour vigil. The old ones are the best . . . though we must admit also having 'mommy' have her spleen

surgically removed is sheer genius.

IS THAT SPILT RINGLY?

Sure the paparazzi are psychopaths, but it's no excuse for bad grammar. Both coverlines about Bo on the scandal sheet they work for say Laramies' rather than Laramie's. Then again, who cares, when the magazine offers classic lines such as 'Laramies Penal Enhancement'?

IT'S ELEMENTARY . . . BUT NOT ELEMENTARY ENOUGH

Dennis Farina's shuffling Columbo-work-a-likey needs to watch a few more episodes of the classic cop show. Columbo surely wouldn't go to all the trouble of getting Bo's fingerprints by stealth and guile, when they would be freely available at HQ after being taken when the 'star' got arrested for biffing Rex.

Cite the Shite

'I'm going to destroy your life and eat your soul.'
Rex, who clearly enjoys his work, makes a promise to Bo

'Nice legs, when do they open?'
Leonard proves the Paparazzi Charm School was worth the money

Make a Shite Night of it

THE TEN COMMANDMENTS ACCORDING TO MEL GIBSON

Despite Gibson being a good Catholic boy and the man who at last brought Aramaic to the big screen in *The Passion of the Christ*, he seems to have forgotten his basic bible class.

In Mel's *Paparazzi* world, the ten commandments have been simplified and shortened. Memorise them and use them as a code to live by.

- If A Man Taketh A Photo Of You, Do Not Turneth The Other Cheek. Punch-eth Him In The Face
- Thou Shalt Not Covet Mel Gibson's Career
- Thou Shalt Not Alloweth Any Man To Taketh Your Wife's Spleen
- What Hollywood Giveth, The Paparazzi Shall Not Taketh Away
- Thou Shalt Not Scene Steal.

ABASCAL SCISSORHANDS

Make the career of director Paul Abascal your specialist

Rex had the money shot, if only he could find his glasses

subject by answering the questions below (answers at the bottom of the page).

1 What did Paul do on the set of *Lethal Weapon 2*?
2 Name Paul's full job title on the movie *Star Trek III*?
3 On *Die Hard 2*, Paul received a promotion, what was it?
4 What did Paul say to Sylvester Stallone on the set of *Judge Dredd*?
5 Paul worked with Madonna on *Who's That Girl?* in what capacity?

ANSWERS
1 Hair stylist.
2 Additional hair stylist.
3 Supervising hair stylist.
4 'Trim sir?' He was Stallone's personal hair stylist.
5 As hair stylist.

THE VILLAGE

2004

What they wasted:
$US 71,682,975

Minutes you'll lose:
103

THE GUILTY
Director: **M. Night Shyamalan**
Lucius Hunt : **Joaquin Phoenix**
Edward Walker: **William Hurt**
Alice Hunt: **Sigourney Weaver**
Noah Percy: **Adrien Brody**
Ivy Walker: **Bryce Dallas Howard**
August Nicholson: **Brendan Gleeson**

TRAILER TRASH
Run. The truce is ending.

I: Let the bad color not be seen. It attracts them.
II: Never enter the woods. That is where they wait.
III: Heed the warning bell, for they are coming.

The Story

Confirming that M. Night Shyamalan-adingdong was a one-twist wonder after *The Sixth Sense*, this story of *Little House on the Prairie* gone bad tries so hard to convince you something astonishing is looming that even the appearance of a huge porcupine in a red dress is anti-climactic.

It's also ludicrous; we're meant to believe that the poor inhabitants of the Village have obediently stayed within the confines of their town for decades simply because they've been told to fear 'those we do not speak of'.

It is only when what looks to be a skinned chihuahua turns up that anyone starts to wonder if something might be amiss. Suddenly an idyllic life of wearing black, having to marry your cousin and never questioning anything is turned upside down as more furless chihuahuas are found and everyone starts jawing about 'those we do not speak of'.

If only the villagers had television, or PS2, or even Barrel O Monkeys, perhaps they wouldn't be over-focusing on the idea there are monsters in them thar woods and would

Joachim touches up his co-star

realise they are all part of Edward Walker's misguided plan.

The 'big' twist – and yes, we are going to tell you – is that he and the other town elders (including a Sigourney Weaver desperate to rub herself up against Hunt's hessian jacket) – have decided to opt out of modern society.

Fair enough, you say, but it is their insistence on making up a silly story about creatures in the woods, colours you can't wear and speaking in 18th century prose that makes *The Village* a square mile of shite.

Imagine it: Edward talks you into moving to the country, next thing you know you are dressing up once a month as Sonic the Hedgehog, talking like Mr Darcy and being banned from owning primary colours.

What keeps you there? Intimidation, fear, the feeling of

impending violence – why not just live in the Bronx? Surely not even the promise of 'magic rocks' to protect you from the porcupines could make the move worth it.

Delight in the Shite

ERETHIZON DORSATUM 'THE ANIMAL WITH THE IRRITATING BACK'

Why does Hurt base his method of crowd control on the harmless porcupine? When attacked, these rodents hide their faces, throw their bellies to the ground and hope for the best. And yet, so terrorised are the villagers they regularly toss the 'monsters' a side of pork, bury anything that is red and wear yellow at night. Apparently all of this goes down well with what must be some very confused porcupines who, obligingly, don't eat anyone.

IN THE TWO- EYED VILLAGE, THE NO-EYES GIRL IS QUEEN

One thing movies tell us over and over again is that blind people are much wiser and kinder than anyone else. They have amazing intuition and can 'see' things we dummies with good vision can't. Hence Bryce Dallas Howard's blind Ivy is a natural choice to be sent into the woods in search of life-saving drugs for her dying fiancé Lucius (Joaquin Phoenix). At least she never has to know she's wearing a mustard hot water bottle cover.

BAD DAD

William Hurt's Edward is a poor choice as village elder. Not only does he keep everyone in a constant state of panic, but he lets Ivy stumble onto the awful truth – quite literally. When he takes her to 'the shed that can't be used' he lets her walk into his costume of 'those we do not speak of'. Despite her amazing blind-person intuition, Ivy gets quite a fright. Why didn't he just say, 'Look Ivy, I've been lying, I've got a big porcupine costume in the shed' instead of putting the fear of God into her?

VILLAGE OF THE DULL

Ten minutes in this village and you'd wish you were being mugged on the streets of L.A. It makes an Amish farm seem like the house of fun. In Hurt's utopia, sweeping the porch passes for an adrenalin rush, running up a hill is the best day out you are likely to get and the only reason to marry is because you can wear a Morris Dancer's hat and do a jig. No wonder someone takes up skinning pets.

UNDERSTATEMENT OF THE YEAR

For a place where nothing ever happens, Brendan Gleeson's elder isn't fazed when he delivers the news to Ivy that Village idiot Adrien Brody has gone berserk and attacked Lucius. 'There's been an accident,' he says. Last time we looked, multiple stabbings didn't come under the heading 'mishap'.

Cite the Shite

'Forgive us our silly lies.'
Let's see – keeping over 100 people in a state of terror for over 20 years . . . No Edward, we don't forgive you

'Please sir, let's make haste.'
The good old, bad old 18th century is back again

'He doesn't joke or bounce about.'
Ivy's sister on Lucius – that makes him the marrying kind around these parts

Make a Shite Night of it

MAKE YOUR OWN VILLAGE
Gather your friends together and break away from society. Before you do, make sure you have some Village-type rules such as:
1 You can only wear plum
2 You must communicate in jazz dance steps
3 No-one can have anything round
4 Everything outside the Village must be referred to as 'all those things that are outside the Village we generally don't mention, and their mates'.

LET'S TWIST AGAIN
Come up with a better twist than M. Night Shyamalan's. For example, the Village is actually in a snow dome that hasn't been shaken for some years.

Shi-fi

Aeon Flux (2005)
Battlefield Earth (2000)
Bicentennial Man (1999)
Catwoman (2004)
Fantastic Four (2005)
The Postman (1997)
War of the Worlds (2005)
Waterworld (1995)

AEON FLUX

2005

What they wasted:
$US 62,000,000

Minutes you'll lose:
93

THE GUILTY
Director: **Karyn Kusama**
Aeon Flux: **Charlize Theron**
Trevor Goodchild: **Marton Csokas**
The Keeper: **Pete Postlethwaite**
The Handler: **Frances McDormand**
Sithandra: **Sophie Okonedo**

TRAILER TRASH
The future is flux.

The perfect world meets the perfect assassin.

The Story

Any movie with a title that evokes an unfortunate recurring digestive disorder surely deserves a place in the canon of shite and *Aeon Flux* does not disappoint; it's sci-fi without sci and only a half-hearted attempt at fi. It's what we like to call *shi-fi*.

Shi-fi is notable for its poorly imagined futuristic worlds, an area in which this film version of the cult comic strip excels; its best 25th century inventions are a dictator named Trevor and a woman who has hands on her feet, which simply can't be convenient in any way, unless you want to knit two jumpers at once or give a particularly enthusiastic round of applause.

Luckily, you don't need feet-hands to get a grip on *Aeon Flux*. It's a movie that conveniently delivers its plot in two bursts – an entrée that sets the scene for how Earth's last city was born, and a quick main course in the middle that explains everything else that has happened since. There's no dessert.

The only danger is that – in between these two bite-sized explanations – you inadvertently spend time believing the various characters who tell us things are 'more complicated' or 'not as simple' as they might seem, and wait for something interesting to happen.

It doesn't. *Aeon Flux* is a movie that figured stitching Charlize Theron into a lyrca jumpsuit would compensate for any inadequacies in the script – like having some words in it. As a consequence, this otherwise 'serious' actress walks around the future as shi-fi's Most Noticeable Rebel.

Indeed, she makes even less of an effort to blend in than a crazed albino monk (see *The Da Vinci Code*, page 24). Not only does she appear to tower over the vertically challenged residents of Bregna like an Amazon on stilts, but she strides about by day dressed in black with a stocking over her head, talking loudly in shopping centres about freedom. She'd be better qualified as a spruiker.

Her lack of super-heroine training also shows in her combat technique; you rarely hear of Navy SEALs or the SAS striking fear into their enemies with impressive displays of cartwheeling.

Then again, perhaps Aeon is exactly the kind of girl you send after a baddie called Trevor – whose main crime

'Look, no hands! No feet!'

turns out to be inventing a mass fertility program to battle post-apocalyptic sterility. As shi-fi's Villain with the Best Intentions, he's been quietly cloning everyone so nobody has to ever be alone.

Perhaps she doesn't want to keep coming back as a bizarrely dressed assassin, but Aeon disapproves of the plan and puts an end to Trevor's big cloning machine in the sky. It's a pity, and not just for poor overworked Trev – we were looking forward to *Aeon Reflux*, a shi-fi classic about one girl's struggle not to keep repeating herself . . .

Delight in the Shite

I, FLY

In the opening scene, Theron's heroine catches a fly with a blink of her eye in her lashes – presumably she has 'no job too small' painted on the side of her van.

MISSION POSSIBLE

Aeon's missions just aren't that taxing. They include pulling the plug out of a big bath, treading on the grass while breaking into Trevor's easily penetrated stronghold – which is so badly defended he might as well leave a key under a pot plant outside the front door – and roughing up her best mate Sithandra (who gets confused by having so many hands and barely lands a punch with any one of them). She's more like a delinquent shoplifter than a highly trained killer.

YOUR BOWELS OR MINE?

How have telecommunications moved forward in the 25th century? Holograms perhaps? Or tiny wrist intercoms? No, if you want to have a chat, it's not as simple as pressing 'speed dial'. Instead, you swallow a pill which then lodges in your stomach and transports your astral body to a meeting with the person you were calling, presumably somewhere in your own bowel. No wonder Aeon has the flux. What's wrong with SMS, or semaphore, or sending a postcard? Lord alone knows how you receive the bill.

FUTURE FASHION

Judging from her clothes, Aeon doesn't get paid much for her tireless work harassing that nice man Trevor – she doesn't have an item in her wardrobe that could be considered complete. Her jumpsuits always have a piece missing, while her choice of sleepwear has been sourced at a string factory. Despite that, the strands of material passing as her clothes must have taken up most of the prop budget leaving poor Pete Postlethwaite, as The Keeper, wearing a brown paper bag and Yoda's forehead.

GINGER-LEADER

Having swallowed one of the phone pills, Aeon invariably ends up trussed up like the Bride of Frankenstein, talking to a small woman sporting a big ginger hairdo that looks as though birds live in it. Frances McDormand's The Handler then proceeds to talk in riddles and dish out orders and even blows poppy seeds in Aeon's eye (luckily, she's been practising catching small things in her mascara and is unfazed). Any self-respecting assassin would surely demand that this mad ginger woman get out of their stomach and straight to a hairdresser.

Cite the Shite

'I like my shoes.'
Aeon comes up with a compelling argument against feet-hands

'I've waited 400 years for this day – I'm tired.'
The Keeper looks forward to finally getting out of his paper bag

Make a Shite Night of it

NEVER LOSE YOUR MARBLES

Aeon declines the use of lasers or light sabres in favour of some performing marbles. Buy yourself a bag and see how long it takes to train them to follow you.

SHOW OF HANDS

Show the movie one evening to friends and amaze them by using your feet as hands. NB: this may not be the best time to serve canapés or take up needlepoint.

BATTLEFIELD EARTH 2000

What they wasted:
$US 73,000,000

Minutes you'll lose:
115

THE GUILTY
Director: **Roger Christian**
Terl: **John Travolta**
Ker: **Forest Whitaker**
Johnnie Goodboy Tyler: **Barry Pepper**

TRAILER TRASH
It's *Mortal Kombat* meets *Independence Day*.

It's time to prepare for battle!

The Story

Subtitled 'a saga of the year 3000', the action unfolds on a future earth ruled by ten-foot tall, dreadlocked, furry-footed aliens called Psychlos. Humans survive in small, semi-feral groups and are used as slave labour in mines. Chief of security, Terl, played by Travolta, tries to teach one of these 'man animals' to speak Psychlo so he can use him to mine gold and make his fortune.

Battlefield Earth, released in 2000, belongs to the 'ego gone mad' genre; a brand of bad movie-making which occurs when a star, unfettered by modesty or reason, loses all grasp on reality. Results of such celebrity self-delusion include dire vanity projects, clucking turkeys and religious treatises like this one.

Devout scientologist Travolta tried for a long 18 years to persuade anyone who would listen to make a movie of scientology guru Ron Hubbard's sci-fi book. Wisely, all the studio bosses got their secretaries to deflect his calls, until *Pulp Fiction* made him too powerful to ignore. Still, Travolta had to put up a large chunk of the budget himself, and co-produce to get this clunker off the ground.

Nothing redeems *Battlefield Earth*. For at least half the movie it's unclear what's happening. Even the overblown orchestral soundtrack appears to have been transplanted from a different movie. The alien villains are lumbering, laughable and one-dimensional – much like the film itself.

Thanks to Travolta's dedication, those with an insatiable appetite for shite can now also learn why hardly anyone takes scientology seriously.

Delight in the Shite

PSYCHO PSYCHLOS

The alien stars resemble an unfortunate combo of the Cowardly Lion, some Klingons and a semi-decomposed Michael Bolton. Their massive, bouffant heads keep hitting the scenery and the long dangly things (they're meant to be breathing tubes) hanging from their noses make you wish their mums had taught them to carry hankies. Instead of terrifying, the Psychlos are deliciously ludicrous.

BATTLEFIELD MIRTH

High camp doesn't begin to describe the strutting, yelling and grimacing that pass as performances in *Battlefield*. Travolta leads from the front, repeating most of his lines twice, adopting a curious, wheedling accent and filling the script's many chasms by shouting 'Ha ha haaaa!' He doesn't just chew the scenery – he swallows it, digests it, regurgitates it, and splatters the result all over his fellow actors.

PSYCHLO-SPEAK

Terl and his pals frequently, and without any warning, lapse into Psychlo, which sounds like someone vomiting underwater. For the first ten minutes or so, they speak nothing else and there are no subtitles. Mel Gibson later expanded this idea into his all-Aramaic *Passion of the Christ* and Mayan *Apocalypto*. No-one stopped him, either.

MAN ANIMALS LEARN FAST

Once free, the ragtag, illiterate bunch of humans stumble upon abandoned, fully fuelled fighter aircraft from centuries ago, and teach themselves to fly them in just a couple of days. From here, it's a small step to their next achievement: destroying a faraway enemy planet.

They fought bitterly over the last hairgrip

THE MAGICAL LEARNING MACHINE

Watch as a bolt of light transforms daft, illiterate Johnnie Goodboy into an intellectual giant. As he hunts rats for his dinner, he tells his pals: 'I've been learning about this thing called molecular biology . . .'

Cite the Shite

'I am a Psychlo of my word.'

So says Terl – but would you trust a man with nose tubes and furry feet?

'We only have seven days to take our planet back!'

Johnnie is prone to panic attacks

'The company requires me to vaporise you.'

Terl, always the company man

Make a Shite Night of it

DIANETICS DINNER PARTY

The Psychlos are aliens so of course, all their stuff is green. Hold a dinner party in which food and drink are entirely green. Experiment with Midori, Crème de Menthe and other green-tinged beverages to achieve the perfect Psychlo beer shade. Tasty treats might include green jelly, pea soup or Thai green curry. Knock back one of your alien cocktails every time Terl sinks a green beer.

HUMANS VS PSYCHLOS STYLE WAR

It's fancy dress, shite-style! Dress as the character of your choice, but attempt to make your costume tackier and poorer quality than its *Battlefield* equivalent. Green prizes can be awarded for most inventive attire. Extra prizes should be given for those brave enough to leave the house in costume. Travolta did, so why can't you?

BICENTENNIAL MAN

1999

What they wasted:
$US 100,000,000

Minutes you'll lose:
131

THE GUILTY

Director: **Chris Columbus**
Andrew Martin: **Robin Williams**
Amanda Martin ('Little Miss')/Portia Charney:
Embeth Davidtz
Rupert Burns: **Oliver Platt**
Richard Martin ('Sir'): **Sam Neill**

TRAILER TRASH

One robot's 200-year journey to become an
ordinary man.

The Story

Buried within this robo-schlock, there's a poignant subtext: the story of Andrew the android is Robin Williams' career in reverse. While the robot strives over 200 years for more facial expressions, greater mobility and better comic timing, Williams has been trying for what seems just as long to immobilise his flexi-face, bag of tricks and gag-happy gabble. This has led only to disaster.

As everyone's favourite 70s alien Mork, Williams built a career on his two chief talents: pulling faces and talking very, very fast while everyone else was speaking slowly. This led many people to believe he actually *was* an alien, particularly when the low-necked fashions of the time revealed a thick covering of body fur.

But while rainbow braces and being manic, perky and hairy can suit the young, they don't age well. In fact, on a middle-aged alcoholic, they seem like a desperate cry for help. So Williams went serious – with horrific results.

Throughout the 90s he became a one-man cheese factory, pumping out pap like *Patch Adams*, *Jakob the Liar* and *What Dreams May Come*, all of which featured him in kicked-clown mode, with moist eyes and downturned mouth. By the end of the decade, he was the Cliff Richard of cinema, with his annual Christmas emissions of housewife-bothering, sentimental schmaltz. *Bicentennial Man*, the culmination of this 20-year journey from Mork to mawk, must have frightened even Williams himself because shortly afterwards, he went ginger and creepy and started playing nutters. But that's another story.

While there is a good argument for putting Robin Williams in a tin can and sealing it for hundreds of years, it doesn't make for quality cinema. The movie is a metal *Mrs Doubtfire*, without the funny frocks and boob jokes. Wearing

A tinder moment

a chrome bodysuit for much of it, Williams plays Andrew, a future family's mechanical manservant. With his shiny, blank face and absence of irony, humour or initiative, Andrew is more pet American than machine, and for this reason the most rewarding scenes are those featuring man's inhumanity to robot – especially the one where children make him jump out of a window. We're supposed to feel sorry for Andrew, but it would be more upsetting to witness a kettle being manhandled. There's just something so utterly unappealing about Williams and his daft chrome dome that you long to feed him into a garbage compactor, melt down the remains and turn them into something useful, like a soup spoon.

Delight in the Shite

FAT SUIT
Robin Williams' chrome costume is a disturbing sight; the robot suit is shaped like late-career William Shatner; wide in the girth, but with a strangely perky bum that makes you feel rather queasy. Obviously the folks who design

Ferraris or Alessi kitchenware were on holiday when Andrew was in production.

FACE-ACHE
When Andrew finally gets the chance to have any human face, does he choose the features of George Clooney or Brad Pitt? No. After 200 years, mankind's crowning achievement is developing the technology to make Robin Williams. God help us all.

THE PERFECT MAN
Quite why Little Miss and then Portia resist the idea of going out with a robot is unclear; women fall for men with no heart and emotions all the time. You'd think they'd welcome the prospect of one who never belched, farted or left stubble in the sink.

METAL FATIGUE
For someone without a personality, Andrew seems to have been made with the selfish-chip firmly in place. Not content with his easy life as a bottle opener with a body, it's always 'I want, I want, I want' with him. He wants to be human, buy clothes, get a girlfriend, have a bank account . . . and when he finally has it all, then he wants to die. You'd pull his plug just to stop the whining.

REMEDIAL ROBOT

When Andrew is delivered to the Martin household, he appears to lack even basic programming: he infuriatingly repeats everything the family says, doesn't understand straightforward commands and is constantly watching the children like some dubious uncle rather than looking after them. Meanwhile, he takes to listening to opera, whittling wood into intricate horse sculptures and constructing complicated timepieces. It would be like buying a vacuum cleaner and realising you have to pick up the dust while it learns the violin and composes beat poetry.

Cite the Shite

'It all sounds so very . . . messy.'
Andrew reviews the script

'A relationship between us would be impossible. It would never, could never, work out.'
Portia understandably baulks at shagging a chrome-covered Robin Williams

'I like you. I even understand you some of the time. But I'm not about to invest my emotions in a machine.'
Portia's obviously never owned a PC

Make a Shite Night of it

TECHNO!

View the movie dressed as your favourite screen robot: the Tin Man, Data from *Star Trek*, Rutger Hauer and Sean Young in *Bladerunner* or Kate Beckinsale in anything. Whoever has the best outfit gets a piece of wood in the shape of a horse.

MAN AGAINST MACHINE

Work tirelessly to transform your toaster into Robin Williams. Then throw it out of the window.

CATWOMAN

What they wasted:
$US 100,000,000

Minutes you'll lose:
99

THE GUILTY

Director: **Pitof**
Patience/Catwoman: **Halle Berry**
Detective Tom Lone: **Benjamin Bratt**
Laurel Hedare: **Sharon Stone**

TRAILER TRASH

From a life that was taken . . . a new one
will be born.

The Story

There are villains who want to take over the world, there are villains who want to destroy the world, there are villains who hijack planes and make unreasonable demands, usually involving bags of cash and a getaway bus.

But villainess Laurel Hedare's fiendish plot in *Catwoman*? Sell bad make-up to women, knowing full well it doesn't really reduce laughter lines and other signs of ageing. No wonder when drippy designer Patience discovers the awful truth behind Hedare's latest batch of night cream, she has Patience thrown down a sewer.

Luckily, being thrown down a sewer is the very best thing that has ever happened to a woman who embraces the smock with an enthusiasm normally exclusive to mothers-to-be during their third trimester.

Of course, Berry is being dulled down so that the transformation into the leather clad super heroine astonishes us all, but it isn't long before you begin to suspect the dulling has worked far too well . . .

As Patience, repeat shite offender Berry is such a wimp it's unbelievable that any self-respecting cat would offer her its litter tray, let alone the chance to look good in leather and the ability to land on all fours.

Berry's *Catwoman* interpretation includes sniffing the air, twitching her head and standing on the back of the couch. She'd be more convincing if she brought up a fur ball.

Even the application of a bondage outfit that Patience presumably had in the back of the wardrobe, just in case she ever needed to go out at night with a whip, can't provide the sexiness and sass required.

Meanwhile, Sharon Stone saunters through her role as a desperate housewife turned evil, like a mannequin being brought to life by stop-gap animation. There are times Shazza seems barely bothered to move, which – if we're feeling charitable – could be explained by the notion she is wearing foundation cream that can stop a bullet.

Cats everywhere will be heading for the cat flap, as this cat flop wends its way to a conclusion with all the energy of a stuffed Siamese. Behold, the shite story of a boring woman who, by night, becomes . . . an annoying woman.

Fluffy had warned Patience about the dangers of too much catnip

Delight in the Shite

LONE COP

There must have been cutbacks in public spending in the aptly named Detective Lone's city, as he appears to be doing the job of ten men; he has to do the school visits, attend robberies, investigate murders and prevent suicides. In fact, you can be sure if you dial 000, Lone will be the first on the scene. Perhaps if he had a little help, he wouldn't take so long to realise the attractive lady he's just started dating is the very same attractive lady who is going about the city at night in a leather bikini. Or perhaps he just assumes everyone else multi-tasks, too.

WHAT CATS COULD DO

Judging from the powers Patience obtains from her feline friends, if cats were human, they could:
• Cut their own hair into bobs
• Use a whip better than an Australian stockman
• Ride motorcycles
• Do martial arts
• Accessorise.

CG –WHY?

Computer Generated Imagery is all too often used for evil and not for good. As Berry's Catwoman leaps from rooftop to rooftop, the CGI makes her look like Gollum on speed. Meanwhile, when the animated

Catwoman is moving slowly, she walks like a cowboy wearing wet underpants.

OLD CATS' HOME

When Patience takes Midnight the cat back home, the house is a small, Victorian mansion smack bang in the middle of the city and dwarfed by the skyscrapers surrounding it. Whenever you see a clearly misplaced house of this kind in a movie it is either the home of a freak, a mad person, an extremely old and wise person or a woman who has 154 cats. Patience really should have seen the catnip bottle coming.

PAWS FOR THOUGHT

She may have received a blow to the wig, but why doesn't Patience at least do some of the things you might do if you woke up on a rock with amnesia and a cat on your chest? Perhaps see a doctor, or even a vet, inform the police (otherwise known in this town as Tom), or mention to a friend that you've started sleeping on top of the wardrobe, can see in the dark and enjoy raw fish?

Cite the Shite

'I was everything they wanted me to be. I was never more beautiful. Never more powerful. And then I turned 40 and they threw me away.'
The only line Stone delivers with passion

'Tom Lone, it rhymes with cone.'
And drone, and moan, and groan . . .

Make a Shite Night of it

CATIKA – THE MOVIE

Take the plots of *Gothika* (see page 94) and *Catwoman* (see page 146) and see if you can make them into one film called *Catika*. Send the pitch to Halle Berry including a key scene in which she cuts her hair and suddenly becomes more attractive. Sign a Hollywood contract and send some of the money to us.

OLD POSSUM'S PARTY OF IMPRACTICAL CATS

Ask your friends round to watch *Catwoman*, but insist everyone must do their own interpretation of a cat throughout the evening. Invite Andrew Lloyd-Webber. And Garfield.

FANTASTIC FOUR

2005

What they wasted:
$US 100,000,000

Minutes you'll lose:
106

THE GUILTY
Director: **Tim Story**
Reed Richards/Mr Fantastic: **Ioan Gruffudd**
Victor Von Doom/Dr Doom: **Julian McMahon**
Ben Grimm/The Thing: **Michael Chiklis**
Sue Storm/Invisible Woman: **Jessica Alba**
Johnny Storm/Human Torch: **Chris Evans**

TRAILER TRASH
Five people will be changed forever. 4 ever.

Prepare for the fantastic.

The Story

Prepare to meet a new breed of superhero. They're not super at all, and they're certainly not fantastic. They're just a terrible nuisance.

Ten years in production, this definitive manual on how not to make a comic book movie features a troupe of spandex-clad misery gutses who are of no use to anyone – even each other. Thrill as the Four annoy passers-by with their bickering! Gasp as they obstruct public highways! Cheer as evil Dr Doom, emerging from a garbage truck, threatens to wipe them out forever!

In a marketplace currently overcrowded with caped crusaders and masked macho men, a superhero movie needs a point of difference to stand out. Director Tim Story (shame he can't tell one) arrives at a novel solution: five of the most dislikeable protagonists you'll see outside a Hitler biopic.

When four space adventurers and their rich patron, Victor Von Doom, are zapped by a cosmic storm, they receive unusual special powers. Scientist Reed Richards becomes the elastic Mr Fantastic; not a 90s Shaggy song but a human rubber band who can 'elongate any part of his body'. Although a career in adult entertainment surely beckons, he prefers to brood at his computer. Sue Storm can become invisible and generate force fields but prefers to tut disapprovingly at her brother Johnny, the only one who likes his new powers. He is now the Human Torch, and sets about using his spontaneous combustion skills to impress chicks and get on TV.

Ben Grimm's giant new persona, The Thing, is a po-faced orange monster no-one loves. He is, however, not an engorged Victoria Beckham but a heap of stones – half Ayers Rock and half vintage cheddar. Instead of seeking out new career opportunities, such as becoming a quarry or a nesting place for seagulls, he mopes around on public buildings while pigeons poo on him. He also doesn't have ears.

As for Von Doom, the cosmic rays appear at first to have bestowed nothing on the movie's bad guy apart from male pattern baldness and an irritable disposition. Later, he turns to steel, performs a weak Darth Vader impersonation and wears a metal mask on top of his metal face. As villains go, he's as threatening as a tulip.

Fantastic Four is the last,

sad, dried-up sandwich left on the superhero buffet table after everyone's been through and taken the Batmans, Spider-mans and even all the X-Men. It's essential viewing for those keen to see the nadir of comic book ineptitude adorned by bad acting and an execrable script. Behold the might of shite!

Delight in the Shite

PESTER POWER

Superheroes are supposed to help society, but the world would be a much safer place without the Fantastic Four. They use their powers almost exclusively to clean up their own damage, starting with The Thing's first super-feat: a traffic pile-up. They're such a public menace, if you were having villain trouble you wouldn't call them – you'd slap a restraining order on them.

MEAN MISSUS

The real villain of this movie is Grimm's inexplicably cruel fiancée. He is the film's nicest guy, but as soon as the missus sees his new craggy face she throws him out. She then hunts him down (after he's saved some lives) just to hurl their engagement ring back in public and watch him try in vain to pick it up with his clumsy big fingers. Clearly, she can't handle a relationship turning rocky. In fact, she vanishes at the first sign of rubble.

COMIC STRIP

Although everyone else's clothes accommodate their superpowers – Mr Fantastic's stretch; the Human Torch's clothes survive flames – the Invisible Woman's garments don't disappear when she does. This means that she has to take them all off in public to vanish properly. As an excuse for nudity (which of course can't be seen anyway because she's invisible), it's pitiful. As a way of adding titillation without jeopardising the PG 13 certificate, it's almost evil genius.

Cite the Shite

'A few days in space. What's the worst that could happen?'
Reed anticipates the making of this movie

'I've always wanted a woman I could give the

world to . . . and in my case, that's not just a metaphor.'
Von Doom will need a lot of wrapping paper

'You could kill yourself, other people, and burn up the atmosphere, ending all human life as we know it.'
Reed was never good in the kitchen

Make a Shite Night of it

NAME THAT FOUR
What would *you* call the super-zeroes? Invent alternatives such as the Nuisance Four and the Miserable and Ungrateful Four, and award an elastic band for the best name.

EVERYONE'S A HERO
Allocate special powers to everyone, and display them throughout the evening. Someone might be good at opening beer bottles with his teeth; another could be an expert at belching. See if you can use your powers for good.

Cosmic radiation left Ben with the strength of ten men and a huge hand puppet

THE POSTMAN

1997

What they wasted:
$US 80,000,000

Minutes you'll lose:
170

THE GUILTY

Director: **Kevin Costner**
The Postman: **Kevin Costner**
Abby: **Olivia Williams**
The General: **Will Patton**
Bridge City Mayor: **Tom Petty**

TRAILER TRASH

Our only hope is an unlikely hero.

The Story

It's 2013. Mankind has survived another one of those apocalyptic disasters that mean everyone has to dress in 80s clothing again. Survivors live in fortified towns, fearing a visit from the local warlord who, frankly, doesn't have very good manners.

There is no central government, not much rain, quite a bit of lawlessness and a lot of deserted American diners. Out of the desolate landscape comes one man who will change the course of history and give the people courage to rise up. That man will be . . . a postie.

That's right. If you thought the title of this movie was a clever metaphor, you were wrong. Although in our own time period we know postmen mainly as dog-bite victims or disgruntled souls who unload shotguns into sorting office employees after a lifetime of simmering disenchantment, the future's saviour is a man with a bag. Cometh the moment, cometh the mailman.

At first, he's an accidental postman – he steals the uniform and van from a skeleton – but soon warms to his role of roaming bullshitter,

convincing people that not only has the United States of America survived (this inexplicably pleases them) but also that they can now enjoy a postal service.

This news particularly delights the masses – they've obviously forgotten what it is to queue in the local post office for hours on a Friday lunchtime, only to be told by a woman with a face like a bag of nails that it's now closed.

But their hunger for bureaucracy elevates the postman to the role of revolutionary leader and he's soon heading a team of teenage posties determined to make the world a better place.

This upsets local military nutter and ex-photocopier salesman The General, and he becomes determined to stop the post getting through. Perhaps

He was a mule for love . . .

he's worried all his unpaid bills will catch up with him.

Meanwhile, in this ponderous vision of the future, Americans haven't changed at all. They're still warlike, racist, given to spontaneous displays of line-dancing and gleefully jingoistic. When a little girl breaks into 'America the Beautiful' for no particular reason, you feel like shoving her into the postie's sack and dumping it in the Mississippi.

Sci-fi has given us Mad Max, Superman and Luke Skywalker. Shi-fi gives us Postman Pat. Worse still, it also keeps on giving us Kevin Costner and his preachy, narcissistic, mullety nonsense. What frightens us most about the apocalypse is that this serial audience-botherer, like a cockroach with bad hair, always seems to survive.

Delight in the Shite

DONATIONS WELCOME

In the future, there's always a shortage: dry land or watery-land, good hair, nice clothes, pastel colours and soap. But the greatest demand of all is for Kevin Costner's sperm. In both *Waterworld* and *The Postman*, Kev only has to look at a local lady and she's after a donation that can't be popped into a charity box. And thus, this particular postman delivers more than the post.

POOR NEWS DAY

For a rudimentary society, the people of the future are prolific letter writers – even the blind ones. What are they scribbling about?

'Dear General, can you please not rape and pillage my village anymore. It unsettles the livestock. Yours etc.'

'Dear Bridge City Mayor, did anyone ever tell you that you bear a startling resemblance to Tom Petty? Yours etc.'

'Dear Postman, could you possibly come round and sleep with my wife? Thank you for your anticipated generosity. Yours etc.'

(blank) Yours, the Village Blind Lady.

WE DO NEED ANOTHER HERO, ACTUALLY

Forget postmen – the future should have been saved by The Milkman. Then the townsfolk could have ordered gold top; ensuring their calcium intake was high and their bones were strong enough to start an uprising against an army which, after all, enjoys watching *The Sound of Music* every night. And milkmen have never shirked at sharing their sperm with a willing woman or two.

BIG FAT FIBBER

Why on earth the citizens venerate the postman so much is baffling. He steals from a dead man, claims Ringo Starr is now President and is so bone idle Abby has to literally set light to his bed to get him out of it. Instead of a statue of him gallantly riding his horse, his memorial should have been a bloke hiding in an old wooden cabin in his vest, pretending to be asleep.

FASHION REVIVAL

At the end of the film we zoom through to 2043 – and everyone's wearing nice, mass-produced T-shirts in bright colours. Obviously the post has started getting through to China.

Cite the Shite

'Ride, Postman! Ride!'
Does Sheriff Briscoe, on his deathbed, suddenly want sperm, too?

'Patton had his Rommel.'
Er, wasn't that Montgomery? The General shows his photocopier-salesman roots

Make a Shite Night of it

SOUND AND FURY

Have your own 'Shakespeare off' just like The Postman and The General. The one to muddle, confuse and make up the most quotes will receive a fan letter in the mail.

AMERICA! AMERICA!

Whenever there is a pause in conversation with your friends or work colleagues, sing a rousing chorus of 'America the Beautiful'. Memorise all eight verses first and insist on going through each one of them. If someone doesn't kill you, you win.

GO POSTAL

Write lots of letters to Kevin Costner politely requesting that he stop making movies. Bugger it; just email him.

WAR OF THE WORLDS 2005

What they wasted:
$US 132,000,000

Minutes you'll lose:
117

THE GUILTY
Director: **Steven Spielberg**
Ray Ferrier: **Tom Cruise**
Rachel Ferrier: **Dakota Fanning**
Robbie Ferrier: **Justin Chatwin**
Harlan Ogilvy: **Tim Robbins**

TRAILER TRASH
This Summer, the last war on Earth won't be started by humans.

They're already here.

The Story

Spielberg's reworking of the HG Wells' classic *The War of the Worlds* provides a night of shite that will have you on the edge of your seat; cheering the action on, biting your nails when all seems lost, closing your eyes in terror at the near misses . . .

At least that's what you'll do if you take the only course possible and throw your support behind the aliens who come to earth and, quite sensibly, start sucking Americans up into a huge blender.

The only other choice would be to try to care about Cruise's deadbeat dad and his two thoroughly annoying offspring – Fanning's pale-but-uninteresting neurotic tween and Chatwin, her testosterone-charged brother who believes his teenage angst is more pressing than the planet being invaded.

Rarely has a movie family been so utterly charmless and lacking in basic common sense. Cruise, as weekend father Ray Ferrier, isn't just irresponsible, he's so dumb that if you left him in charge of amoebas, they would outwit him and run away. Indeed, if the movie's central theme of survival of the fittest was faithfully applied, Ray would be extinct before the end of the opening credits.

His first act of genius occurs when a huge black storm darkens the horizon, complete with winds higher than his pants. Run indoors? Hide in the cellar? No! Send the 12-year-old out to watch the ensuing tsunami in the garden.

Not content with that, Ray then rushes to the storm's epicentre and stands, peering into a huge crater. When cars begin flying through the air, Ray hides behind . . . a car.

As his efforts to return his kids to their mother in Boston continue – for some reason he thinks the aliens won't go to Boston – Ray lets his son drive the only functioning car in America into an angry mob who are keen for a ride, then loses his revolver and puts his life in the hands of Tim Robbins' lunatic who has managed to go native in his own basement.

All of which Ray does accompanied by the white noise of Fanning's constant whining, while the highly evolved invaders repeatedly fail, for some unfathomable reason, to put an end to a family whose gene pool could easily be mopped up with a Jiffy cloth.

Aliens in every solar system would watch this, beat their chests with their three-fingered hands and wail: 'why, oh why, oh why?' in whatever system of clicks and whistles they speak. No matter what galaxy you are in, there just isn't a satisfactory answer.

Delight in the Shite

SEEN AND UNFORTUNATELY HEARD

What exactly is wrong with Fanning's 12-year-old? Her mother and stepfather seem perfectly stable, and she only spends the rare weekend at Ray's tip. Yet Rachel flies into hysterical screaming when he puts her in the car and can only be calmed by her brother's life coach-style instructions when he tells her to make a ring with her arms and repeat 'I am safe in my space'. Although these children have never witnessed an alien invasion before, they have clearly seen every episode of *Dr Phil*.

BLINDING IDEA

When Ray decides that his only choice is to beat Harlan to death rather than simply make his polite excuses and leave the basement, he blindfolds Rachel before going into a separate room to do the unnecessary deed. It must be another of Ray's survival-defying ideas – if Harlan were to win, poor little Rachel literally wouldn't see him coming.

ALIENS R US

Like most sci-fi movies, *War of the Worlds* presents us with aliens who seem entirely ill-suited to either travel or oppressing other planets. In case you spot something in the sky, remember:
• Aliens are always extremely cumbersome, usually with only three fingers and no opposable thumbs (something even Ray has)
• They build their sophisticated space ships to resemble themselves, which is a bit like manufacturing a line of tanks in the shape of Dakota Fanning
• They are highly evolved life-forms, but if you hide round a corner, they'll never find you.

MOB RULE

Even though the aliens are clearly looking for large, slow-moving crowds, one of Ray's best ideas is to hook up with a slow-moving crowd heading across a choppy Hudson River on a small ferry. They'll never find him there.

WALL OF SHAME

When the family comes across the Hudson River ferry, they see a wall that already has posters on it about missing people. The crisis is no more than 12 hours old and yet the first thing Americans do when facing invasion is grab the Uhu stick, take the family album to the nearest photocopying machine and start pasting pictures on public boards.

Cite the Shite

'I've got a busy day ahead of me.'
Cruise's mechanic mate sees dollar signs where there is only genocide

They couldn't remember how long they'd been waiting to jump out and shout 'Surprise!'

'This came from somewhere else. . .'
'Europe?'
Good guess . . .

Make a Shite Night of it

PSYCHOBABBLE

Come up with your own 'safe in your space' catchphrase that you can use if aliens invade, or Dakota Fanning comes round to visit. We like: 'I am in Bora Bora,' or 'I am George Clooney's underpants'.

FOLLOWING ORDERS

Make an application to the American army listing all of Robbie's skills, including listening to iPods, slamming doors, joy-riding and running away. See how quickly you get promoted – prepare to be frightened.

GO ALIENS!

Get your friends to get behind the alien invasion by making banners with slogans such as 'Kill the Ferriers'. Watch the movie, waving them and shouting encouragement to the invading force. Who knows, maybe your collective will can change the ending.

WATERWORLD

What they wasted:
$US 172,000,000

Minutes you'll lose:
136

THE GUILTY

Director: **Kevin Reynolds (then Kevin Costner)**
Mariner: **Kevin Costner**
Deacon: **Dennis Hopper**
Helen: **Jeanne Tripplehorn**
Enola: **Tina Majorino**

TRAILER TRASH

Beyond the horizon lies the secret to a new beginning . . .

The Story

Much has been written about *Waterworld* since it plopped forth over a decade ago, but nothing says it quite as eloquently as this water bomb's own opening scene: Kevin Costner drinking his urine. Right from the very first frame, this vanity-crazed actor/director is taking the piss.

Once again, we witness that peculiar madness which sends a megastar's ego spiralling so far out of control no land mass can contain it. When this happens, the only way to go with your movies is away from reality and off to other planets (see *Battlefield Earth*, page 138), dimensions, eras, and sometimes away from film altogether and into bad music (Russell Crowe).

In this case, Costner's runaway vanity was so buoyed by standing behind Whitney Houston a lot in *The Bodyguard* and then dancing with wolves for more hours than anyone ever should, it headed out to the open seas and left the shores of sense far behind.

During Kev's odyssey, he fired director Kevin Reynolds and took the helm himself, steering *Waterworld* into budget blowout and absurdity. At the time, it was the most expensive film ever made, and this lends grandeur to its failure. It's epically awful; a big, bloated *Ben Hur* of badness.

Costner drips his way around screen as a moist Mad Max called Mariner, a surly amphibian in a flooded post-apocalyptic world. Even for a man with a waterlogged wardrobe he is a right sight, with his wet-look mullet, earrings and complicated leather accessories. If it weren't for the gills and webbed feet you'd mistake him for a rain-damaged member of Def Leppard.

Being part man, part tuna and part puffin can get you into all kinds of trouble; women want to steal Mariner's sperm so their children will inherit his Ian Thorpe-like swimming skills, men want to dangle him in cesspits and Helen (Jeanne Tripplehorn) insists on sharing his boat and moving his plants around. Mariner's perpetually furrowed brow, monosyllables and short temper might just have been Costner's signature acting style, but they more likely betrayed his growing realisation that this disaster at sea, along with his other 90s howlers, *Robin Hood: Prince of Thieves* and *Wyatt Earp*,

As hard as they looked, none of them could see their next career move

completed that decade's most outstanding hat-trick of shite.

It's quite an achievement. Although perhaps not for the reasons its makers hoped, this unwieldy floater will remain forever wedged in the U-bend of cinematic history.

Delight in the Shite

SPLASHING OUT

The $US172 million dollar question is: what did they spend the money on? The sets look as if your dad knocked them up in his shed one Sunday afternoon from a pile of hubcaps, and the wardrobe is a charity clothing bin. Either Kev awarded himself Hollywood's largest ever pay rise, or the entire movie was filmed in tanks of Evian.

DROWNED PRATS

In the future, nature's laws are topsy-turvy: only the stupidest survive. Humanity's finest include a woman who can't swim despite being born on a waterlogged planet and a man wearing a colander to keep the rain out. Everyone keeps whingeing about living on water, but is it really so hard? We've got one word for the people of *Waterworld*: Venice.

HELLO SAILOR

We reckon Mariner has a secret, but it isn't the route to Dry Land. Clues: he's obsessively house proud and sulks when visitors rearrange his boat and mess with his pot plants, he's the only seaman ever to refuse free shags with the ladies in port, and when Enola makes fun of his mullet he flies into a tantrum – then punishes her by giving her a bad haircut. In short: he's a bit festive.

MUDDY WATERS

The people of *Waterworld* become over-excited by thoughts of dirt, and hysterical when they actually see a pot of it – and yet they're covered in the stuff. If they all had baths they could build themselves a new country from the tidemarks left around the tub.

THINGS THAT SURVIVED THE GREAT FLOOD

Dennis Hopper's fags and lighter
This villain may not be able to locate Dry Land, but he knows where the cigarette machine is.

A Jack Daniels factory
Water, water everywhere . . . and yet all the bottles of whiskey you can drink.

Hair products
You don't get volume like that in a damp climate without chemical help.

Guns and gunpowder
Despite the wet, Waterworld's gangsters are packing fully functioning firearms, not water pistols.

The 80s
History's most resilient fashion moment defies the odds once again. Elaborate hair and fussy clothes prevail where utilitarian essentials have failed to survive.

Cite the Shite

'Nothing's free in Waterworld.'
As the studio's accounts department discovered

'All we want is your seed.'
It's unclear whether the women of *Waterworld* want to grow tomatoes or make babies

'Don't just stand there – kill something!'
Dennis Hopper realises the extras have blown the budget

Make a Shite Night of it

SOMETHING FISHY

Throw a *Waterworld* pool party. If you don't have a swimming pool, use an inflatable paddling pool. Serve only seafood, and drink only Jack Daniels. You may, of course, smoke.

DRIP IN THE OCEAN

Everyone watches *Waterworld* with their feet in a bucket of water. The one with the most wrinkled feet at the end of the movie wins a tub of dirt.

Singa-longa Shite

Glitter (2001)
Phantom of the Opera (2004)
Rent (2005)

GLITTER

What they wasted:
$US 22,000,000

Minutes you'll lose:
104

THE GUILTY

Director: **Vondie Curtis Hall**
Billie Frank: **Mariah Carey**
Julian 'Dice' Black: **Max Beesley**
Rafael: **Eric Benet**

TRAILER TRASH

In music she found her dream, her love, herself.

A strength to survive. A desire to dream.

The Story

If you've ever considered fame beyond your reach, take heart from this rags-to-riches tale based upon Mariah Carey's own life. *Glitter*, the easiest hard luck story you'll ever see, proves the road to success is littered not with adversity, but minor irritations. It also reminds us again that pop singers and movie cameras shouldn't be allowed in the same country as each other.

It's a long way to the top – unless you're Billie Frank. After an inauspicious start as the abandoned, mixed-race daughter of a drunken lounge singer, our heroine sets out to chase her dream of becoming a famous singer. Except she doesn't chase it so much as assume the appearance of a dazed chipmunk and wait for it to drop like a stray acorn into her lycra-clad lap, which it very quickly does.

Amid the obstacles Billie encounters along the way – a date that isn't really a date, some pleasant dreams, a mildly annoying publicist and a boyfriend with an unsightly medallion – the most significant setback is a French video director who uses too many shiny bits in a promo. 'The glitter can't overpower the artist,' we're warned, as Billie's perma-beam threatens to falter at this crisis.

As Carey smiles her way from poverty to global success using just a squeaky voice, pigtails and a series of forgettable songs, we can only wonder why she ever needed to be hospitalised for 'exhaustion' in real life. According to her biopic, superstardom requires less effort than a toilet visit after a vindaloo.

The movie delights with all kinds of little mysteries: why is it the 80s? Why does white Dice talk like a black man? Why does Billie still live in a modest, one-room apartment after achieving global mega-stardom? Why doesn't she know how to work a telephone – even a big orange one? You can lie awake at night trying to unravel the puzzle that is *Glitter*.

Critics declared this one of the worst films ever made, and it almost certainly is. But we believe there is something awe-inspiring and immortal about a disaster on this scale, like the Titanic or the Hindenburg. Glittering it ain't, but this diva-saster of a movie shines like a dazzling star in the great constellation of shite.

Delight in the Shite

RAW TALENT

Despite everyone's assurances she's got 'that special something', Billie's only discernible skill is a tendency to warble in the melodic stratosphere. These unnerving vocal stylings sound like an enraged Flipper the dolphin or anything else that makes you put your fingers in your ears.

MAKIN' SWEET MUSIC

How do you seduce a laydee when you're a tough-talkin' DJ with muscles and a porno wardrobe? Play the xylophone! Billie's boyfriend, Dice, chooses the world's naffest instrument to serenade her and it must work, because she immediately strips down to massive knickers behind a frosted window. Later, she honours Dice's memory by performing a forgettable song they wrote together telepathically while in separate houses.

SLUMMY MUMMY

Glitter begins with Billie's deadbeat mum dumping her in an orphanage, promising she'll retrieve her when she stops being poor and pissed.

Decades later Billie finds Mom, not slumped in a gutter but residing in a luxury country pile. The scorned daughter reacts with – what else? A cheeky chipmunk smile.

BILLIE'S SIX STEPS TO SUCCESS

Follow the *Glitter* plan for overnight stardom:

1 *Own an immortal cat*
Billie's ginger puss first appears at the orphanage and ten years later is un-weathered by time. Perhaps he's stuffed, or wandered in from *Catwoman* (see page 146).

2 *Have friends in formation*
When times get tough, it's essential to have pals who dress in matching colours and dance with you through the streets in a row. It helps if they're from comedy minorities.

3 *Squeak*
The higher the voice, the closer to God. And people will pay you just to go away.

4 *Get giant pants*
The higher the knickers . . . etc. With granny pants, you'll create a memorable silhouette wherever you go and always be visible – even through semi-opaque surfaces.

5 *Smile*
. . . even if something terrible happens, like living in the

world's friendliest orphanage, or being chatted up by a rich superstar.

6 *Love your mum*
Even if your mother looks like post-drugs Whitney Houston and always tries to avoid you, be nice to her.

Cite the Shite

Billie: 'You know, I don't usually do this.'
Dice: 'I can tell.'
After sleeping with Dice, Billie pretends she didn't put those big knickers on to seduce him

'I don't soup girls up.'
Dice prefers to woo with xylophone tunes

'We ask ourselves, is she black? Is she white? We don't care. She's exotic. I want to see more of her breasts.'
A video director attempts to define Billie's special something

Make a Shite Night of it

SINGALONGAMARIAH
Join in all the songs. You may employ artifical aids, such as helium or a blow to the crotch, to achieve Mariah's top notes. Alternatives: a dog whistle, old-fashioned kettle or fretful baby.

WHOSE LIFE IS IT ANYWAY?
Take it in turns to think of individuals blessed with more fortunate lives than Billie Frank. These might include lottery winners, royalty or the pampered pets of rich people.

NAME THAT TUNE
Split into pairs and, with each of you in a separate room, jointly compose your own telepathic melody. Perform the songs. Best effort wins a pair of big knickers.

As the glitter rained down, Billie held on to her big knickers

PHANTOM OF THE OPERA

2004

What they wasted:
$US 60,000,000

Minutes you'll lose:
135

THE GUILTY

Director: **Joel Schumacher**
The Phantom: **Gerard Butler**
Christine: **Emmy Rossum**
Raoul: **Patrick Wilson**
Madame Giry: **Miranda Richardson**
Carlotta: **Minnie Driver**

TRAILER TRASH

The waiting is over . . . let the fantasy begin.

The Story

With *Moulin Rouge* and *Chicago* providing a groundswell of interest in singing and dancing in recent years, reports of the death of the musical seemed premature yet again.

The trouble is, the moment this once glorious genre looks to be resurrected, out comes Sir Andrew Lloyd Webber waving a dated stage show at Hollywood and insisting there's life in his Casio yet (he hasn't even pressed a lot of the rhythm section buttons).

And so, around 30 years after the Broadway hoopla has vanished, we get *Phantom of the Opera* – the Movie. On the upside, Sir Andrew of Cliché couldn't persuade a popstar to star in it – J-Lo wasn't available and Britney didn't want to do Oprah.

But that's the only upside, as the overblown theatricality of the stage production turns into an overblown, theatrical film production populated by actors so wooden you're not sure who is wearing a mask and who isn't.

One person definitely in a mask – well, half a mask – is the Phantom himself, played by the little known Gerard

No-one knew, but he was laughing on the other side of his face

Butler. He lives beneath the famous Paris Opera House and frightens the patrons with disembodied voices and scuttling about the gods.

While it would take Velma from the Scooby gang about two minutes to work out he's a deformed crank, show people tend to be slow people, and they firmly believe he's a ghost.

The slowest of them all, Christine (Emmy Rossum), goes one plot device further, thinking he is her dead father who has been giving her free 'beyond the grave' singing lessons since she was about 11.

Imagine her shock (actually, you'll have to, because Rossum's face doesn't really move) when she discovers he is an ugly bloke with a chip on his shoulder and a comb-over who has spent years living beneath the opera house in what appears to be Disneyland's 'It's a Small World After All' ride but with more candles and fewer dolls.

What's so shite about it all is that the Phantom is a better catch than Christine's thick-necked, long-haired Count (Patrick Wilson). After all, despite having spent his life in a basement, the Phantom is a self taught architect, designer, musician and magician. Judging from the amount of water in his gaff, he's not much of a plumber, but you can't have it all.

And so the entire premise of the movie rests on the fear Christine will be held captive forever by an extremely erudite and talented man. He'd be sending her back upstairs within minutes.

Delight in the Shite

MONTHLY SHOP

Every month the Phantom gives a shopping list to Madame Giry. Judging by the décor in his subterranean pad it includes: Candles, more candles, white flowers, a doll's house, bridal wear, mirrors, more mirrors, wax, a gondolier, one horse.

Giry is a very resourceful shopper.

THE LIGHTS ARE ON . . .

. . . but there really isn't anyone home. Right up until the end Christine believes the Phantom is really her 'angel of music'. All he has to do is tell her 'The phantom of the opera is there, Inside your mind', and she figures it must be true. If all this becomes arduous, she just nods off – even if it is mid-dance with a maniac. Why on earth he wants her as a lifetime companion – Lord alone knows. He doesn't get out much.

DECISIVE. MAYBE

Christine's low IQ strikes again when Raoul overpowers the Phantom in the graveyard (she thinks taking a walk in a misty, remote graveyard when a nutter is stalking you is a grand idea) and is about to run him through. Instead of letting Raoul do it, and thus saving us all from another half an hour of warbling, she stops the Count with 'No, not this way.' Then *how*? Tying his shoelaces together when he is at the top of the grand stairway? Chucking an electric toaster in his bathtub? Leaving him in the library with a service revolver and hoping for the best? Even the Fantastic Four (see page 150) would have opted for a swift offing while they had the chance.

POSITIVE THINKING

If only the Phantom spent less time on opera and more time reading comic books, he'd know that having a special gift and wearing a mask aren't necessarily negatives – look at Batman, Zorro, Spider-man and Joan Rivers.

UNION DISPUTE

When it comes down to it, this whole mess arises from a labour dispute. For spicing up their operas, the Phantom believes he should be paid 20,000 francs by management, have his own private box and that Christine should be promoted to lead singer. It's nothing John Howard's new Workplace Relations Act couldn't have solved swiftly and decisively.

Cite the Shite

''ana I ate my 'at.'
Minnie Driver's authentic Italian accent

'Down once more to the dungeon of my black despair!' 'Down that path into darkness deep as hell!'
Phantom-speak for 'I'm just nipping downstairs'

'Angel of Music, you've deceived me. I gave you my mind blindly.'
Christine, offering an empty gift

Make a Shite Night of it

RSVP

To prove he is a good catch, post the Phantom's details on RSVP.com and see how many responses he gets. Don't use a photo just yet.

QUEER EYE FOR THE DEFORMED GUY

Devise a Phantom makeover to make him attractive to women and transform his home into a friendlier, less damp and more practical space. Once you've finished, turn your attention to Quasimodo's bungalow and the Elephant Man's beach house.

RENT

2005

What they wasted:
$US 40,000,000

Minutes you'll lose:
135

THE GUILTY
Director: **Chris Columbus**
Marc Cohen: **Anthony Rapp**
Roger Davis: **Adam Pascal**
Mimi Marquez: **Rosario Dawson**

TRAILER TRASH
No day but today.

The Story

If you thought musicals could only be about deformed cranks in opera house basements, epic love stories or Argentina, then welcome to *Rent* – musical history's most mundane score murdered by a cast that resembles the kids from *Fame* if they'd been chucked out for pulling Mr Shorofsky's white hair and nicking Leroy's leg warmers.

In this modern day updating of *La Bohème* and – mystifyingly – hit Broadway show, the list of topics thought worthy of lengthy musical discussion include a candle repeatedly blowing out, the difficulties of setting up a sound system and, of course, how annoying it is to have to pay rent when you are bone idle. All earnestly explored with lines as lyrically complex as One, Two Buckle My Shoe.

'Who do you think you are/Barging in on me and my guitar?' warbles mullet-headed Roger. 'Ever since puberty/Everybody stares at me,' whines bisexual performance artist Maureen. 'I had it when I walked in the door/It was pure – is it on the floor?' complains wimpy Mimi about her lost drugs. 'We're not gonna pay/Last year's rent! This year's rent!/Next year's rent,' they all howl.

After half an hour of hearing them making up songs – apparently on the spot – about their minor domestic disasters, you'd happily see them thrown out onto the street if it didn't mean they would start trilling at innocent people who do have jobs, such as commuters and waiters. In fact it's a waiter who evokes our sole sympathies during this litany of fuss-about-nothing when he pleads: 'No, not tonight,' as the gang burst through the doors of his restaurant and proceed to harass other diners, dance on the table and bellow more dire ditties.

The only hope for a respite from rhymes such as 'pookie' and 'spooky' is when Roger announces he is heading off to New Mexico ('It's true you sold your guitar and bought a car?' asks Mimi, pleased that she's found another word to rhyme with 'guitar').

It's Roger's dream to write a brilliant song (he presumably finds New Mexico inspiring). Lord knows, if he'd pulled it off, it would be the first in the entire musical.

Unfortunately, as we discover to our horror when he gets

there – in a car, no guitar – Roger's strategy involves standing around like a poor man's Jon Bon Jovi who's been driven out to the desert, spun around lots of times and left to make a pop video.

By this time, you have the answer to the opening refrain about how you measure a year in someone's life: with this lot, very, very slowly.

Delight in the Shite

NOT-SO-SAD-FACE
To cheer up the perennially miserable Roger, his mates decide to take him out to an HIV support group, in which the members repeatedly intone: 'Will I lose my dignity?

The Christmas elf from hell . . .

Will someone care? Will I wake tomorrow from this nightmare?' over and over. It would have been more therapeutic for poor Roger to stay home in the dark and repeatedly smack his head against the cold, peeling walls of his unpaid flat.

GET A JOB!
No matter how many times they warble on about their impending financial ruin and lack of rent money, none of the unemployed yobs figures out the obvious solution – get jobs. Then they could sing heartily about getting up in the morning for work, having chats around the water cooler and counting paperclips.

SCROUNGER'S SERENADE
When Collins falls for Angel he declares his love by singing: 'Open your door, I will be your tenant.' Now Angel really should know better than to believe it. If anyone's learned anything from this movie so far, it's that no-one in it has the slightest intention of paying a dime in rent.

BAD CAREER MOVE
Anyone who knows a lawyer will understand that hanging around with a gang of wasters, activists and drug addicts isn't exactly the fast track to a senior partnership. Why does

Harvard graduate Joanne want to associate with this bunch of miscreants? Surely it can't be so she can listen to Maureen's captivating conversation – 'Moooooooo, Moooooooo, Moooooooo, Moo with me Moo yes! Moo YES! Moo with me!' – every night before bed.

LYRICAL MIRACLE

Although all she ever does is whine, Mimi's mates spend weeks looking for her when she disappears – presumably she gets lost in the dark. They eventually find her and rush her not to the nearest hospital, but to the damp industrial building Roger mopes around in. Once they've deposited her upon the kitchen table, they decide against calling for a doctor and instead hope she can be revived by the single song Roger has managed to write in the desert. Amazingly, while it is unlikely to make the charts, it can cure pneumonia in minutes.

Cite the Shite

'I teach computer age philosophy, but my students would rather watch TV.'
Perhaps they just want Collins to stop singing

'It's like I'm being tied to the hood of a yellow rental truck being packed in with fertiliser, and fuel oil. Pushed over a cliff by a suicidal Mickey Mouse.'
Maureen describes how it feels to watch *Rent*

Make a Shite Night of it

BECOME YOUR OWN ROCK OPERA

Give your life grandeur by singing it, *Rent*-style. Leave no activity or thought, no matter how dull or minor, unexpressed by crap musical rhyming. Remember: making a cup of tea, going to the bathroom or feeding the budgie can be the stuff of arias and anthems, and you may even win a Tony award.

FREELOAD FOR FUN

Tell your landlord or bank manager you can no longer pay your bills because you are (a) too bohemian (b) not long for this world (c) on drugs (d) lazy, then see how long you can maintain your lifestyle.

Acknowledgements

With thanks to . . . Leigh at the beginning of the Shite, Emma Kean for proofreading Shite, Mags King for finding all the Shite photos, and to the publishing pixie, for appearing and then disappearing just as mysteriously.